WORKING WITH CHILDREN AND FAMILIES SEPARATED BY INCARCERATION

A Handbook for Child Welfare Agencies

Lois E. Wright
Cynthia B. Seymour

FUNDING PROVIDED BY
The Hite Foundation

CWLA Press • Washington, DC

CWLA Press is an imprint of the Child Welfare League of America. The Child Welfare League of America (CWLA), the nation's oldest and largest membership-based child welfare organization, is committed to engaging all Americans in promoting the well-being of children and protecting every child from harm.

CHILD WELFARE LEAGUE OF AMERICA, INC.
440 First Street, NW, Third Floor, Washington, DC 20001-2085
E-mail: books@cwla.org

CURRENT PRINTING (last digit)
10 9 8 7 6 5 4 3 2

Cover design by Jennifer Geanakos
Text design by Pen & Palette Unlimited

Printed in the United States of America

Library of Congress Cataloging-in-Publication Data

Wright, Lois, 1942–
    Working with children and families separated by incarceration : a handbook for child welfare agencies / Lois Wright, Cynthia Seymour.
        p.   cm.
    Includes bibliographical references.
    ISBN 0-87868-783-1 (alk. paper)
    1. Children of prisoners—Services for—United States.   2. Children of prisoners—United States.   3. Prisoners' families—Government policy—United States.   4. Prisoners—United States—Family relationships.   I. Seymour, Cynthia.   II. Title.

HV8886. .W75 2000
362.7—dc21
                                                                    00-037866

Contents

List of Tables and Figures

Chapter 1

Introduction

More than 1.9 million children in this country have a parent in prison, and a much larger number have experienced the incarceration of a parent at some point in their lives. As a result of parental incarceration and the crimes and arrests that precede it, thousands of children have endured traumatic separations from their parents and erratic shifts from one caregiver to another. As a group, these children are far less likely than their peers are to succeed in school and more likely to succumb to substance abuse, gangs, and delinquency. The child welfare system, charged with protecting vulnerable children and promoting family stability, will continue to be significantly impacted by the increasing number of children with incarcerated parents.

Why This Handbook

This handbook has grown out of the Children With Incarcerated Parents initiative of the Child Welfare League of America (CWLA). The initiative arose when CWLA member agencies began to see increasing numbers of children with parents in prison. The enthusiastic response to our initial workshops and publications convinced us that the field wanted and needed more information about this special population. In 1997, we surveyed state child welfare agencies to discover the extent of their knowledge of parental incarceration and what programs and services they currently offered. The survey results demonstrated a dearth of responsive policies and services, but an eagerness for information and assistance. With support from The Hite Foundation, we decided to develop a resource handbook that would highlight the unique service issues surrounding parental incarceration and suggest ways of enhancing child welfare policies and practices to better meet the special needs of these children and their families.

Handbook Goals

The goals of this handbook are to:

- raise awareness in the child welfare community about the needs of children with parents in prison;

- alert agency administrators and caseworkers to the importance of developing policies and programs that are responsive to the needs of those children;

- alert agency administrators and caseworkers to the importance of working collaboratively across systems to meet the needs of children and families separated by incarceration; and

- provide administrators and caseworkers with suggestions for enhancing case management and permanency planning work with children who have incarcerated parents.

The most important message of this handbook, though, is that a parent's incarceration can be a time of opportunity for the parent, child, and caseworker. Typically, parental incarceration is not an isolated incident, but a symptom of more complex family problems. For a caseworker, the period of incarceration provides an opportunity for assessment of at-risk children and families, identification of broader family issues, and comprehensive intervention. The parent is accessible, sober, and often motivated to improve her life. For a parent, incarceration can be a time when, despite formidable obstacles, she can develop new and better relationships with her children, leave behind painful and defeating lifestyles, and participate in programs that help her to be a better parent and a happier, more productive person. For children, despite the pain and loss associated with separation, it can be a time for developing a stronger relationship with a mother or father who is sober, motivated, and better able to be a loving and supportive parent.

Handbook Focus

The issues surrounding parental incarceration are complex, and no one system can single-handedly meet the needs of these families. While this handbook will focus on children with parents in prison who are in need of child welfare services (and CWLA is committed to enhancing child welfare services to children with parents in prison), we recognize that improved child welfare services are not the answer to all of the problems these children face. Many of the children affected by parental incarceration do not and should not ever come into contact with the child welfare system. For this reason, CWLA is also committed to reaching out to professionals in other disciplines who have contact with these children and participating in the creation of a collaborative, multi-system response.

The handbook is primarily focused on children with incarcerated mothers. From a practical perspective, these children are most likely to need child welfare services. Most children with incarcerated fathers are being cared for by their mothers and were not living with their fathers prior to their incarceration. We recognize, however, that there are many more children in this country with incarcerated fathers, and we strongly support the need for child welfare professionals to work with these fathers and promote healthy father/child relationships. Much of what is said about incarcerated mothers, however, can also apply to incarcerated fathers, and we will address some issues unique to these fathers.

Organization and Approach

This book is written for both child welfare administrators and caseworkers. It will discuss the effects of parental incarceration on children and families, the systemic response to parental incarceration, and the community services available to support and preserve these families. It will also outline child welfare practice needs and provide practice suggestions in areas such as child protection, temporary care in out-of-home placements, permanency planning, and family reunification.

While many of the suggestions in this handbook are practice-oriented and focus on what workers can do to enhance the services they provide, we want to emphasize that real change cannot occur unless administrators and agency heads are committed to addressing the issue of parental incarceration. Workers won't be able to take on this challenging service population until agencies adopt and endorse formal policies and procedures to structure, guide, and enforce casework practice, and agency administrators provide necessary training and other resources.

Children and families have long struggled with the difficulties created when a parent goes to prison. Until recently, though, it has not been recognized as a discrete issue warranting special attention and concentrated intervention. It is our hope that this handbook will prompt discussion among child welfare professionals about the impact of parental incarceration on children, will provide suggestions for policies and procedures to enhance services to these children and their families, and will function as a resource to the child welfare community as it responds to growing numbers of these children.

Chapter 2

Defining the Problem

The child welfare field is just beginning to address the issue of children with incarcerated parents. Though the problem was beginning to receive attention in the 1960s (Cassel & Van-Vorst 1961; Zalba 1964; and Ward & Kassebaum 1965), since that time the numbers of investigators studying the issue have been few and the visibility of the issue low. Why have the child welfare and corrections systems previously neglected this special population, and why the attention now?

A number of factors have kept this population hidden from the child welfare and corrections systems. These include a corrections system struggling with its own emerging and ongoing issues (e.g., security, overcrowding, HIV population) and lacking a tradition of taking inmates' children into account in any formal manner; public attitudes toward incarcerated individuals and a negative perception of them as parents; an overwhelmed child protection system, already challenged to serve other emerging populations (e.g., substance-affected infants, seriously emotionally disturbed children) and not eager to take on more; lack of common data bases and the low level of communication between the prison and child welfare systems, so that each is unaware of families' involvement in the other system.

This picture is beginning to change. In the past two decades, due partly to stricter sentencing guidelines and mandatory sentences, particularly in drug-related offenses, we have seen a steadily increasing and changing prison population, in that greater numbers of women are being incarcerated, leaving more children in need of alternative care arrangements. At the same time, we are seeing heightened awareness of and efforts toward intersystem collaboration for more holistic, family-focused approaches to an array of social problems. Meanwhile, stepped-up advocacy for incarcerated parents and their children has helped focus us on this special group with unique needs.

This chapter will present an overview of incarceration in the United States, address what is known about the population of incarcerated parents and their children, and describe why incarcerated parents and their children are a child welfare issue. The limitations in available data are apparent—figures may refer to inmates of federal prisons, state prisons, or local jails; reporting is for various years; and often estimates are used due to the lack of available hard data. Despite these limitations, the story the data tell is clear.

Incarceration in the United States

The 1960s began a period of deinstitutionalization based upon notions of civil rights, the high cost of institutional care, and possible negative effects of prolonged separation of children and adults from family and society. Yet despite a national philosophy and practice of deinstitutionalization, which has dramatically reduced the number of residents in mental health facilities and encouraged community-based care options special needs populations, our country continues to lock up lawbreakers at an alarming rate. Table 1 shows the number of inmates in the United States during a recent nine-year period (1990-1998).

These figures show:

- an increasing numbers of inmates across all categories of incarceration—federal, state, and local;

- an average annual growth in the prison (federal and state) population of 6.7%, with a range from 8.7% (1994) to 4.8% (1998), and 6.5% in the total incarcerated population.

A recent Bureau of Justice Statistics Bulletin (Gilliard & Mumola 1999) also provides additional information about this population.

- At year-end 1998, women comprised 84,427 (6.5%) of the prison population. While the report did not address women in local jails, if the percentage of women versus men in jails is similar to that in prisons, we can estimate that 38,510 women were in jail at the end of 1998, for a total of 122,937 incarcerated women.

- While the percentage increase for male prisoners during 1998 was 4.7%, the increase for female prisoners was 6.5%. Since 1990, the annual growth rate for male prisoners has averaged 6.6%, while the increase in women prisoners has averaged 8.5%.

- There is disparity according to race and ethnicity: in 1997 the incidence of incarceration (federal and state) of males per 100,000

Table 1. **Inmates of the Correctional System in the U.S., 1990–1998***

Year**	Federal***	State***	Local***	Total
1990	65,526	708,393	404,320	1,178,239
1991	71,608	753,951	426,497	1,252,056
1992	80,259	802,241	444,584	1,327,084
1993	89,587	880,857	459,804	1,430,248
1994	95,034	959,668	486,474	1,541,176
1995	100,250	1,025,624	507,044	1,632,918
1996	105,544	1,077,824	518,492	1,701,860
1997	112,973	1,131,581	567,079	1,811,633
1998	123,041	1,178,978	592,462	1,894,481

*   Gilliard and Mumola 1999. Figures are compiled from this report, U.S. Dept. of Justice Office of Justice Programs, Bureau of Justice Statistics Bulletin, August 1999.

**   Figures for federal and state prison are end-of-year (December 1); figures for local jails are midyear (June 30).

*** Figures for federal and state confinement refer to incarceration in prisons, which generally house inmates serving sentences of more than 1 year. Figures for local confinement refer to incarceration in jails, which typically hold persons awaiting trial or sentencing, awaiting transfer, or with sentences of a year or less. These figures do not include nonconfined persons under the supervision of the correctional system though probation or parole.

among African Americans was 3,253; among Latinos, 1,272; and among Caucasians, 491.

• While the growth in the male prison population was primarily due to violent offenses, the growth of the female prison population was due to drug offenses (38%).

These figures provide a sobering picture of incarceration in the United States. We see a pattern of continuing growth in the numbers of incarcerated individuals; increasing incarceration of women, particularly due to drug offenses; a high percentage of inmates serving sentences of over one year, which means an extended period of interruption in family and community life; and disproportionate incarceration of minorities.

A March 1994 Bureau of Justice Statistics Bulletin provides further information about these incarcerated men and women, focusing on a state prison population and using 1991 figures (Snell & Morton 1994). Many—56% of men and 45% of women—never married. In terms of education, fewer than a quarter of state prison inmates were high school graduates (22% men and 23% women). Only 12% of the men and 16% of the women had some college education. In terms of employment, 32% of the men and

53% of the women were unemployed at the time of their arrest. Regarding income, Harlow (1998) states that among men and women incarcerated in local jails in 1996, almost one-half reported incomes of under $600 in the month before their arrest (i.e., under $7,200 per year) and only one-third reported incomes of at least $1,000 per month (i.e., $12,000 per year). In addition, about 22% reported receiving one or more kinds of financial support from the government.

As Table 2 shows, "married" is the least frequent family status, and over one-half of the inmates of state prisons have never married. However, various studies have estimated that 11% of jailed mothers have common-law relationships (Johnston 1995b). Thus, the percentage in a committed relationship of some sort is higher than the married percentage of inmates would indicate.

Table 2. **Marital Status of Adults Incarcerated in State Prisons***

Marital Status	All	Men	Women
Married	18%	18%	17%
Never married	55%	56%	45%
Divorced, separated, or widowed	27%	26%	38%

* (Beck 1992); (Snell & Morton 1994).

Data on inmates' family histories show that at least one member of the immediate family had been incarcerated for 37% of the men and 47% of the women. For approximately 27% of the men and 34% of the women, a parent or guardian had abused drugs or alcohol while the inmate was growing up. Physical or sexual abuse was experienced by over one in ten of the men and over four in ten of the women. Of those who experienced abuse, the abuser was an intimate for 3% of the men and 50% of the women. In addition, Harlow (1998) reported that 48% of women incarcerated in jails in 1996 had been physically or sexually abused, and 27% reported had been raped. Over one-third of men and women in jails in 1996 reported physical or mental problems, and one-quarter reported having been treated for mental or emotional problems (Harlow 1998).

Alcohol and drugs were factors in the lives and crimes of many inmates, as shown in Table 3.

While more than two-thirds of all inmates used drugs regularly and more than one-half used them in the month before their current offense, the percentages of drug-involved women were higher than men. In addition,

Table 3. **Drug and Alcohol Involvement of State Prisoners***

Type of Involvement	Men	Women
Used drugs in the past	83 %	84 %
Used drugs regularly (once per week or more for at least a month)	69 %	74 %
Used drugs in the month prior to the offense	56 %	62 %
Under the influence of drugs at the time of the offense	32 %	40 %
Ever had a "binge drinking" experience	42 %	30 %
Under influence of alcohol at time of offense	38 %	29 %
Committed offense to get money to buy drugs	17 %*	24 %*
Ever used a needle to inject drugs	24 %*	34 %*
Ever shared a needle	12 %*	18 %*
Among those tested for HIV and reporting the results, HIV-positive	2.1 %*	3.3 %*

* (Mumola 1999), (Snell & Morton, 1994)

while around one-third of all inmates were under the influence of drugs at the time of their current offense, this was truer for women than for men.

Table 4 presents data related to inmates' criminal careers and current sentences. More than one-half of the incarcerated men and slightly fewer than one-half of incarcerated women have a history of violence, and men are more likely than women to have juvenile records. Recidivism is high for both groups, as 81% of the men and 72% of the women had prior sentences (incarceration or probation). Though we know that men are more apt to commit violent crimes, women's violent crimes are much more apt to be against someone with whom they are in a close relationship (36% versus 16%).

Thus, adding to our previous picture, we see that incarcerated men and women are apt to be poor; to be undereducated and underemployed; to be single, divorced, separated, or widowed rather than married; often to have family histories marked by substance abuse, physical and sexual abuse, and incarceration of another family member; to be substance involved themselves; to have prior offenses and recidivism; and often to have physical or emotional problems. In addition, women are more likely than men are to have family histories of drug abuse and physical and sexual abuse, particularly from someone close to them.

While this picture of incarceration in itself may be viewed as a significant societal problem, our speczific concern here is with how incarceration affects family life and child rearing in particular.

Table 4. **Criminal Careers and Current Sentences of Inmates***

Characteristic	Men	Women
Of those serving sentence for violent offense, violence was against someone close	16 %	36 %
Of those serving sentence for violent offense, violence was against a stranger	51 %	35 %
Previous sentences to incarceration or probation	81 %	72 %
Prior offenses		
one or none	39 %	51 %
two or fewer	55 %	66 %
History of violence	6 in 10	4 in 10
Criminal record as a juvenile	4 in 10	2 in 10
Sentence length		
less than 36 months	12.4 %	24.2 %
36-59 months	15.0 %	18.7 %
60-119 months	22.3 %	20.5 %
120-179 months	13.2 %	11.9 %
180 or more months	27.9 %	17.7 %
life or death	9.2 %	7.0 %

*(Snell & Morton 1994)

Incarcerated Parents

As we begin to describe the problem of incarcerated parents and their children, the first problem we note is the lack of reliable data. Simply put, we don't know who they are. There are no national policies and few, limited state guidelines concerning the correction systems' responsibility to inquire about the parental status of men and women who are incarcerated. Usually, upon arrest, the officer will ask about children, but formal policies are often lacking. In addition, there are no standard data keeping guidelines or procedures concerning parental status. Thus, it is difficult to profile these parents or to provide accurate numbers. However, reasonable estimates can be given, and certainly we know the numbers are increasing, in keeping with the overall increase in numbers of incarcerated individuals, particularly women.

Men and women in prisons are apt to be of an age most likely to have minor children. In 1997 the modal age group was 30-34 years (19.2%) with slightly fewer in the 25-29 years age group (18.5%), again slightly fewer in the 35-39 years age group (17.5%), and slightly fewer in the 20-24 years age group (15.8%) [Gilliard & Beck 1998]. In fact, it is estimated that 49% of men incarcerated in federal prisons and 55% in state prisons have minor children; and that 59% of women incarcerated in federal prisons, 65% in state prisons, and 70% in jails have minor children [Greenfeld & Snell 1999]. Thus, incarcerated women are somewhat more likely to report having minor children than are incarcerated men.

In addition, child care arrangements differ depending upon whether the incarcerated parent is a mother or father. Ninety percent of incarcerated fathers report that their children were living with their mother, while only 25% of mothers report that children are living with their father (Beck 1992).

These figures provide a beginning look at incarcerated men and women as parents, a perspective too often forgotten, and help us begin to understand that incarceration is a family affair.

Incarcerated Fathers

In 1997 an estimated 1,699,312 men were incarcerated in federal and state prisons and in jails. As we have already seen, these men tended to be poor, undereducated, and underemployed; had family histories of substance involvement, crime, and violence; themselves had histories of substance abuse, violence, and repeat offenses; were apt to be unmarried; and were over-represented by minorities. Now we see that incarcerated men are also likely to be fathers of minor children. For the most part, these men continue to be viewed by their families and to view themselves as parents. Some were active parents before incarceration, whether or not they were married to or living with the mother of the children. Others never learned how but want to refocus on their children during the period of incarceration.

The children of these men are most apt to be in the care of their mothers, who generally provide some support for the father's role, struggling to ensure ongoing contact between children and their incarcerated fathers. However, transportation and communication difficulties, lengthy sentences, or repeated incarcerations can make it so difficult to maintain a paternal role, contact may be broken and relationships fractured.

Incarcerated Mothers

In 1997 an estimated 115,917 women were incarcerated in federal and state prisons and local jails. As we have seen, these women's characteristics and backgrounds are similar to those of incarcerated men, except that their families are more apt to be crime- and substance-involved and to have abused them. In addition, their crimes are less likely than men's to involve violence and more likely to be drug-related. The fact that their violence tends to be against intimates suggests that they often may have been defending themselves in abusive relationships.

It has been estimated that around two-thirds of incarcerated women are mothers of minor children [Greenfeld and Snell 1999]. Unlike incarcerated men, whose children are usually living with their mothers, incarcerated

11

women leave their children in the care of the father only approximately 25% of the time. Thus, finding a care arrangement is a much greater issue for mothers than fathers. In addition, ensuring ongoing parent-child contact is more difficult than when the father is incarcerated, because there is less likely to be a caregiving spouse who will take responsibility for visitation.

As with fathers, parenthood is an ongoing concern for these incarcerated women. In fact, their issues are even greater, because usually they do not have the security of knowing the children are with a spouse, and often living arrangements and even custody issues are uncertain. Their concerns include such things as financial arrangements, decision-making regarding their children, and providing nurturing. In addition, some women enter prison pregnant—an estimated 6 % of those in jail and 5% of those in state prison [Greenfeld & Snell 1999]—and 9% of incarcerated women gave birth to a child while incarcerated [Bloom & Steinhart 1993].

Children with Incarcerated Parents

Data on children with incarcerated parents are even more difficult to access than on the parents themselves, though the number has been estimated at 1.9 million (Greenfeld and Snell 1999). Estimates of age, gender, and race/ethnicity are displayed in Table 5. Most (75% of the children of incarcerated fathers and 89% of the children of incarcerated mothers) are under 12 years of age. For both fathers and mothers, the greatest percentages of children (42% and 46%) fall within the 7–12 years age group. The children are slightly more apt to be girls than boys (52% versus 48%); and they are more apt to be African-American (43%) than any other race or ethnic origin.

We have said that children of incarcerated fathers are most likely to be left in the care of their mother, while children of incarcerated mothers are more apt to go into another care arrangement. Table 6 presents further detail on children's care arrangements. For both incarcerated fathers and incarcerated mothers, the second most likely care arrangement is with the child's grandparent, though for children of incarcerated fathers this is a relatively small percentage (14% and 10%), while for mothers it is the most-used arrangement (54% and 50%). Children of incarcerated mothers are also more apt to be in the care of other relatives, friends, or formal substitute care. (Note: percentages exceed 100%, because some parents will have children in more than one care arrangement.)

Clearly a central issue around children with incarcerated parents is who will care for them. The needs for basic parental support—both material

Table 5. **Characteristics of Children with Incarcerated Parents***

Child Characteristic	Percentage
Age of child(ren) of incarcerated men	
0-6	33 %
7-12	42 %
12-18	25 %
Age of child(ren) of incarcerated women	
0-6	43 %
7-12	46 %
12-18	11 %
Gender of children	
girls	52 %
boys	48 %
Race of women's children	
black	43 %
white	24 %
Hispanic	21 %
Asian, Native American, and other	12 %

* Hostetter and Jinnah (1993).

Table 6. **Care Arrangements of Children During Parental Incarceration***

Care Arrangement	Federal	State	Local
Incarcerated fathers reporting at least one child living with			
Child's mother	91 %	90 %	
Child's grandparent	14 %	10 %	
Other relative or friend	5 %	3 %	
Substitute care*	1 %	2 %	
Incarcerated mothers reporting at least one child living with			
Child's father	33 %	25 %	24 %
Child's grandparent	54 %	50 %	50 %
Other relative or friend	44 %	24 %	27 %
Substitute care*	6 %	10 %	8 %

* Hostetter and Jinnah [1993]

and emotional—continue; their ongoing developmental needs proceed; in addition, the events of crime and incarceration pose new coping challenges. We must be concerned about who is minding the children.

It is also clear that, against the background of the characteristics of incarcerated men and women in general, while all children with incarcerated parents are at risk, the fate of children with incarcerated parents is related to which parent—mother or father—is incarcerated. Looking at care arrangements before incarceration, we find that at the time of a mother's incarceration, chances are she has custody of her children (80%–85%), provides primary financial and emotional support, and plans to reestablish a home with them upon her release (78%). Looking only at state prisons, 7 in 10 mothers were living with their children prior to incarceration. Of fathers, 5 in 10 were living with their children prior to incarceration. Thus, incarceration of a mother presents a greater disruption to a child's living arrangement than the incarceration of a father. Discrepancies continue when we look at living arrangements of children during parental incarceration.

In summary:

- The likelihood of a parent having a child living with the other (non-incarcerated) parent is much greater if the father, rather than the mother, is incarcerated.

- Mothers are much more apt than fathers to rely upon grandparents, other relatives, and friends to provide care.

- Five to six times more mothers than fathers have at least one child in substitute care (foster home or institutional setting).

- Incarcerated parents often have multiple children living with different caregivers.

We don't know much more about this population. Most of these children are hidden, not routinely identified by any agency, and only a small percentage come to the attention of the child welfare agency. The additional information we do have about them—the effects of parental incarceration and their service needs—we know either anecdotally or through small studies. These are discussed in the next chapter.

Incarcerated Parents and Their Children: A Child Welfare Issue

It is not known when and why these children come into care—as a result of abuse or neglect prior to the parent's incarceration, as a direct result of the primary caregiving parent's arrest, or a result of inadequate caregiving arrangements during a parent's incarceration. Although society should be concerned about all the children of incarcerated parents, and certainly all our health and human service institutions, organizations, and agencies—e.g., schools, mental health agencies, health departments—should have heightened sensitivity to this population, child welfare has a special responsibility for those children who come into custody of the state because of maltreatment or lack of suitable custodial arrangements. In addition, many children living with relatives or friends will need supportive services that they can only receive through the child welfare agency.

We have seen the large percentage of children who are living with a relative or friend, particularly when a child's mother is incarcerated. While many of these children are receiving stable and nurturing care, others are at risk of placement disruption if their fragile care arrangements should unravel. We have also seen a small but important percentage of children who are placed in formal substitute care arrangements—foster care or group care. These figures are estimates, however, as we have little information about the percentages of children in our substitute care system who have incarcerated parents. A 1997 CWLA survey revealed that most state child welfare agencies did not systematically capture data on parental incarceration [CWLA 1998], though workers might capture this on a case-by-case basis.

Regardless of numbers, we must consider the seriousness of the problem and the enormous vulnerability of these children. Their parents have family and personal histories (histories of poverty, drug involvement, criminal activity, and recidivism) that don't bode well for effective parenting without significant intervention. We will see in later chapters the potential effects of some of these factors, in addition to the effects of parental incarceration itself, on children. We will also address the opportunity for using the period of incarceration constructively for both parent and child, as well as the enormous obstacles to doing so.

In short, parental incarceration is a serious problem about which we are currently not well informed and which we currently are ill-equipped to address due to the lack of adequate collaborative efforts of the correctional and child welfare systems. It is past time to change that.

Chapter 3

Effects of Parental Incarceration on Children and Families

The exact number of children with incarcerated parents in this country is unknown, since we lack standard procedures for collecting and recording this information, and estimates vary. One estimate placed the number at 1.9 million [Greenfeld & Snell 1999]. In addition, with the incarcerated population growing, these numbers will increase, and with the numbers of incarcerated women growing, more of these children will be left with inadequate care arrangements.

Despite the large and increasing numbers of incarcerated parents, the children have been a forgotten population, their special needs inadequately understood or addressed. Because the corrections system does not recognize these children and because their care arrangements are often handled informally by family, they may never come to the attention of an agency. Moreover, while the children affected may be having problems at school or in other aspects of their lives, these problems may not be recognized and documented as related to the incarceration of a parent. However, at other times—because of abuse or neglect or the inability of the parent to arrange and maintain adequate childcare informally—the children will come to the attention of the child welfare agency. When such children do come to our attention, we must be prepared to understand and help others understand the trauma they have experienced in order to respond appropriately.

We also must be prepared to help those children's families. Because the family—however defined and however reconstituted during the period of incarceration—is the child's primary environment, with potential for either benefiting or endangering the child, it is essential that we become more attuned to how incarceration affects families and support them during their period of transition.

Effects on the Children

Despite the inadequacy of our data on these children, the limited research, taken together with our theoretical and empirical knowledge of similar populations, can provide us with some understanding of the effects of parental incarceration on children.

What Children Experience: Accumulation of Risk

It is exceptional for a family to experience incarceration in the absence of other difficulties. More often than not, an array of social, cultural, and familial risk factors coexist, each adding perhaps only a small increment to the totality of risk for the child and family. Though no one factor is predictive of particular child difficulties, we can predict bad outcomes from an accumulative array of factors; generally, the more endangering factors, the greater the risk. (This is not to say that bad outcomes are inevitable, and resilience within children with incarcerated parents remains largely unexplored.)

It is unclear to what extent the problems experienced by these children are attributable to the incarceration itself—and the resultant parent-child separation—or are more closely tied to factors such as poverty, parents' criminal behaviors, and/or inability to provide appropriate parenting prior to incarceration [Seymour, 1998].

Thus, to understand the effects of parental incarceration on a child, we must look at the totality of a family's experiences involving a multiplicity of interrelated social, cultural, and familial factors, making it difficult to sort out the results of crime, arrest, and incarceration from ongoing life problems. Thus far, research has shed little light on this complexity, and the extent to which child difficulties are tied to factors apart from incarceration itself remain unexplored.

To begin to understand these children's difficulties, we must look at their experiences both before the incarceration and during the incarceration. Though some children may have enjoyed a fairly stable and nurturing preincarceration family life, most will have experienced considerable instability and possibly maltreatment, with the difficulties related to incarceration superimposed upon existing difficulties. Some of the risk factors occurring both before and during incarceration are:

- **Poverty.** Parents are apt to have been living in poverty before their incarceration and to have been unable to provide basic material resources. Poverty is often the core issue for a range of other difficulties that have consequences for children, including living in impoverished neighborhoods, limited parental educational achievement, and limited parental job prospects.

- **Alcohol and other drugs.** Substance use and abuse is associated with poor neighborhoods, child maltreatment, and other social ills, severely limiting the user's ability to function appropriately across a range of life roles. Substance abuse usually has a role in the incarceration, either as a causal factor or the primary offense. Even without the additional problems created by arrest and incarceration, "a mother's drug addiction can undermine her ability to provide consistent nurturing to her children" [Katz 1998].

- **Crime.** Living in an environment of ongoing criminal activity, either the parent's own crime or crime in the neighborhood, has documented effects on children, as they may live in constant fear or may have become numb, accepting danger as a normal part of growing up.

- **Intrafamilial violence.** The parent may have been battered or a batterer. If the mother's partner is currently abusing her, her children are likely to be exposed to that violence at home [Davis 1990, Katz 1998]. Witnessing battering has been documented to negatively affect children (e.g., fear, guilt, and desensitizing to violence) [Carlson 1996].

- **Child maltreatment.** Abuse or neglect of a child for some period before incarceration or as a precipitating factor in the incarceration is well documented as having a range of effects on children.

- **Previous separations.** The children may have experienced previous foster care or other separation, and this period of incarceration may represent one more separation, though one with a slightly different meaning. Still, an ongoing pattern of instability leaves children more vulnerable to effects from additional separations.

- **Parent's history of abuse.** The parent him/herself may have been maltreated as a child, and this experience can affect parenting abilities [Davis 1990, Katz 1998]. Abused parents who have not had the opportunity to deal with their own histories of child abuse or to recognize the ways it might affect how they raise their children may have an impaired ability to provide nurturing and discipline.

- **Enduring trauma.** Enduring trauma is not a separate risk factor but rather a term used by The Center for Children of Incarcerated Parents to describe the multiple and ongoing traumatization some children experience throughout one or several life stages, with no recovery time or supportive resources between traumas [Johnston and Carlin 1996].

- **Arrest and incarceration.** The parental arrest and incarceration expose the child to additional risks: further separations from the parent and possibly siblings, unstable care arrangements, uncertainty about his or her future, secrecy and deception regarding the incarceration, stigma, and difficulties with visitation.

Children's circumstances will vary, and each may experience a unique combination of risk factors. In addition, each child will react differently to his or her experiences, and available services and supports for each child vary. These differences complicate our ability to understand children's reactions to parental incarceration.

Children's Reactions

Despite the limitations in our knowledge of this population and the difficulty of establishing cause-effect relationships amid the potential multiplicity of risk factors, we do have a beginning body of knowledge about some of the negative consequences. Studies have indicated some child difficulties that may be related to the incarceration itself and that distinguish this group of children. We will review here some more general findings (i.e., effects that are similar to those of other forms of trauma) as well as those specifically linked to parental crime, arrest, and incarceration.

As a general context for looking at children's specific reactions to parental incarceration, it is important to understanding the following:

- Children are diverted from development tasks when they experience trauma. It is normally expected that children's emotional energy will be invested in mastering their age-specific developmental tasks (i.e., forming attachments and developing trust, developing autonomy, developing initiative, learning to work productively, and achieving identity). The everyday challenges children experience, if they have the coping resources to meet them, make children stronger and move them forward developmentally. But if the challenges are too great and exceed children's capacity to cope, emotional survival begins to take precedence over mastery of developmental tasks, and they begin to show developmental delays (e.g., retarded language development) or regression (e.g., soiling or clinging), as well as other inappropriate coping strategies (e.g., numbing).

- Children's response to trauma will vary according to age. For instance, Johnston [1992] found disorganized feelings and behaviors in early childhood and maladaptive behaviors in later childhood (i.e., antisocial behaviors such as lying and stealing, aggressive or isolated behavioral disorders, conduct disorders, and depression).

Among older children, sexual misconduct, truancy, delinquency, substance abuse, and gang activity were found [Johnston 1992]. In addition, children of different ages vary in terms of coping ability. Young children are least likely to have acquired the developmental skills necessary to cope with trauma and will be most in need of intervention. If they are unable to respond adaptively, they will respond maladaptively [Johnston 1992].

- Children's reactions will vary over time. While we lack longitudinal studies documenting how children's reactions change over time, we know generally that a crisis reaction is different from a long-term accommodation (adaptive or maladaptive) to trauma. In addition, we know that intervention is more effective if it is offered before maladaptive patterns have settled in and begun to feel "normal" for the child. Theory related to the grieving process suggests that people go through stages of grieving; these children are grieving for the absent parent. While the pattern of reaction is not invariable and the theory not entirely substantiated, it does provide some guidelines for understanding changing reactions over time. In addition, long after the traumatic event, posttraumatic stress reaction has been observed in some children [Johnston 1992].

- Children are always traumatized by separation. Regardless of the cause of the separation (e.g., parental death, divorce, military service, incapacity, or incarceration), it has a profound effect. These effects on children of different ages have already been well documented in the child welfare and divorce literature. We know that, depending upon the child's age and length of separation, reactions can include such things as inability to form later attachments, woebegone searching, numbing, self-blame, anger, depression, regression, and antisocial behaviors.

- Children's abilities to cope are hampered by uncertainty. While coping with bad situations is difficult, coping with uncertainty (e.g., relatives missing in action or abducted) is even more difficult. Yet uncertainty pervades the child's life when a parent is incarcerated, touching basic life issues. Answers to questions such as "what is going on?" "where will I live?", "who will care for me?", "when will I see my parent again?", "when will she/he be home again?", "will there be enough money?", and "what will happen next?" remain nebulous. The child enters a period of remarkable instability and uncertainty, not even knowing with what he or she must cope. Often, a caregiver's well-meaning attempts to deceive the child only serves to increase the child's stress.

- Children's trauma due to parental incarceration has some unique features. Sometimes the parent's crime is actually against the child, as in the case of severe physical or sexual abuse. The child may have witnessed a crime (including murder) by one parent against another. The child might have witnessed other types of criminal activity or been solicited for involvement in criminal activity (considered emotional abuse). Thus, it may pit family member against family member, undermining the child's sense of safety, security, and loyalty to a parent.

- Children suffer stigma when a parent is incarcerated. For most, stigma is everywhere—in the community, among peers, and often in their own extended family—causing feelings of shame and low self-esteem. For other children, coming from neighborhoods or families in which incarceration and related trauma are everyday events, stigma is not a great factor [Gaudin & Sutphen 1993; The Osborne Association 1993]. These children's lives are already seriously disrupted, however, and the fact that they experience less stigma than others is no gift.

- Children express their distress through their bodies. Most children will find it difficult to communicate their distress through words, unless there is strong support for doing so. Rather, they express themselves through physical, emotional, cognitive, and behavioral means that we call symptoms.

The following chart presents some of the physical, cognitive, emotional, and behavioral reactions that have been noted in children with incarcerated parents, although age-specific information was unavailable. There was no attempt to connect any aspect of trauma with any one symptom. Instead, we must realize that these reactions are interconnected, as feelings may spring from thoughts, and behaviors may result from feelings, and they usually, though not always, appear in constellations.

In addition, posttraumatic stress reaction is receiving increasing attention. When children have been exposed to multiple and ongoing traumas, such as seeing a parent arrested, unstable care arrangements, secrecy, and stigma, they may begin to show a constellation of symptoms that comprise posttraumatic stress disorder (PTSD). Symptoms may include depression, sleep disturbance, anger, fear, daydreaming, problems in concentration, preoccupation with events surrounding the trauma, and hearing the parent's voice [Kampfner 1995].

Table 7. **Child Reactions to Parental Incarceration**

Child Reactions	Source
• Identification with incarcerated parent, awareness of social stigma	[Gabel 1992]
• Change in future orientation and intrusive thoughts about their parents	[Kampfner 1990 in Johnston 1992]
• Concerned about outcomes of case, unsure and worried about how to live without mother, concern about an uncertain future	[Children with incarcerated parents, Gabel & Johnston 1995]
• Flashbacks to traumatic events related to arrests	[Kampfner 1995 cited in Beckerman 1998]
• Embarrassment and anger	[Hannon et al. 1984 cited in Beckerman 1998]
• Fear, anxiety, anger, sadness, loneliness, guilt, low self-esteem, depression, emotional withdrawal from friends and family	[The Osborne Association 1993]
• Separation anxiety, emotional withdrawal, guilt	[Johnston 1995c]
• Depression	[Kampfner 1995]
• Abandonment, loneliness, sadness, anger, resentment	[McGowan & Blumenthal 1978, Henriques 1982, Hungerford 1993, cited in Block & Potthast 1998]
• Eating and sleeping disorders	[Rocheleau 1987 cited in Block and Potthast 1998, p. 565]
• Aggression, anxiety and hyperarousal, attention disorders and developmental regression	[Sack et al. 1997, Stanton 1980, Henriques 1980, Fritsch & Burkhead 1982, cited in Johnston 1992]
• Physical aggression, withdrawal, acting out, academic and classroom behavior difficulties, truancy	[Johnston 1995c]
• Acting out inappropriately, disruptive in class, other antisocial behaviors	[Gabel 1992]
• Diminished academic performance, disruptive behavior at home and school	[Stanton 1980, Zalba 1964, Henriques 1982, Hungerford 1993, cited in Block & Potthast 1998]
• Sleeplessness	[Kampfner 1995]
• Aggressive and trauma-reactive behavior leading to early crime involvement	[Johnston 1995c]

Effects on the Family

It is important to look at the effects on the family, because that is the primary environment of the child, providing support and protection or exposing the child to threat and endangerment. As the previous discussion has shown, many families experience ongoing difficulties—poverty, instability, violence, and substance involvement—upon which the crisis of crime and incarceration is superimposed. How is the family different from before these events? The primary changes can be categorized as structural, material, emotional, and dynamic, though these actually interact, each impacting the other.

Structural Changes

Perhaps the most immediately apparent change in a family is structural. A family member is now absent, and either a remaining family member must take on the departing parent's roles and responsibilities, or those roles remain unfulfilled. Either scenario produces stress on the family.

Though most incarcerated men are either single or divorced, with fewer than one-fourth being married, most have children in whose lives they have played some part prior to incarceration [Hairston 1998]. Usually, because the father is seldom the sole caregiver of a child, the children continue to live with their mother. Still, the incarceration, whether the father was a full-time member of a household or a nonresident contributor, does remove him from whatever roles he may have filled in his child's household (and some fathers leave several households behind, as they have fathered children by several women). The roles may have included sole or partial breadwinner, nurturer, physical caregiver, disciplinarian, and general companion to share the tasks of family life. Even if there were negative aspects to his presence in the family (as there may have been if there was a history of family violence, substance abuse, or crime), the father's absence leaves a hole that the mother must struggle to fill.

Because the mother is more likely than the father is to be the custodial parent and primary caregiver of a child, her incarceration will most likely have an even greater effect on family structure. If she has run an independent household, her children will need new living arrangements. Usually her children will stay with a relative, most often the maternal grandmother. The caregiver's home will also experience structural change through the addition of the children, so children may find themselves living in a home that has been disrupted by their presence, even though they may be wanted there. Sometimes one caregiver is not able to care for an entire sibling group, so brothers and sisters may be separated. This separation only contributes to the trauma and disorientation that children experience when mothers become incarcerated.

In some cases, the mother has lived in a three-generational household, or the child has already been spending most or all of his or her time with the relative. In such a case, the incarceration will still change family structure. With the total absence of the mother from the household, family rules, roles, and relationships will shift, and the entire family must adjust to these changes.

Material Changes

Incarceration occurs disproportionately for families who are already living in poverty [Johnston 1996] and poses further financial difficulties. If a father is incarcerated, child support (court ordered or informal help) will be interrupted, possibly plunging the family into financial crisis. If he is the sole support of his family, the mother may have to go to work, which will have structural, emotional, and dynamic reverberations. If a mother who is the primary caregiver is incarcerated, the children may be left with no means of financial support except what can be provided by the substitute caregiver, often with state assistance.

If the substitute caregiver is a relative, most likely a grandmother, she may be unprepared for the financial effect of taking on a new child or children. Meeting children's needs is not without cost, and the older the child, the greater the cost. Like the child's parents, the caregiving family may already be living at or below the poverty level, and the new responsibilities may strain the family's capacity to function. If the child is young, the relative may have to quit work to provide care or pay expensive day care. Paying for telephone calls and visits to the incarcerated parent is an added expense, and the child's problems may necessitate special treatment services for which the family is unable to pay.

Emotional Changes

The whole family may go through an emotional upheaval as they experience the stigma, shame, guilt, and pain of dealing with a family member's incarceration. Dealing with the criminal justice system—the lack of information about how to contact the parent, conditions surrounding visits, uncertainty about what will happen to the parent—involves additional stress. While some families will cope admirably well, others may cope by expressing anger at the parent or insisting on secrecy about the incarceration. Sometimes they exclude the incarcerated parent from the family life altogether, which may protect them in the short term from having to deal with their feelings but unfortunately interferes with the maintenance of parent-child ties and exacerbates problems around reentry when the parent is released.

Dynamic Changes

Over time, families work out ways of coping with incarceration, but the change always affects family dynamics and ongoing psychological patterns of relatedness. Different communication patterns may emerge, old family issues may resurface, new coalitions may be formed, and power in the family may shift. As the family system feels increasingly stressed, it is not uncommon for one family member to become the symptom carrier for the family, acting out everyone's distress. This person can be identified as the "problem" in the family and sent for treatment, yet it is difficult for him or her to give up symptoms unless the whole family is involved in the treatment. Incarceration can precipitate a period of great instability in a family, and unless members understand what this can do to family dynamics, they may turn their anger and blame on one another, and the family may crumble, leaving the children exposed and vulnerable.

Meaning for Child Welfare

It is important to reemphasize that some families will have experienced few of these factors. Perhaps for them the parent's crime and incarceration were fairly isolated incidents in otherwise stable families. We can't stereotype these families, which are as different from one another as any group of families would be. Just as multiple factors combine to pose risk for children and families, so multiple factors can influence eventual positive outcomes. Yet most children and families, particularly those that become known to the child welfare system, experience considerable difficulty.

Thus, child welfare needs to target children of incarcerated parents as a special population requiring special consideration and services. Remembering that a safe and stable family is the first line of prevention and treatment for a child, we must support the child's caregiving family, whatever that may be. In addition, we must understand and provide whatever special treatment the children may need. Much of the remainder of this handbook deals with how we can work with incarcerated parents, their children, and their caregiving families to ensure children the best chance of overcoming the tremendous odds they face.

Chapter 4

Systemic Response

We have already seen that the populations served by the criminal justice and the child welfare systems overlap. The two populations share many characteristics and are sometimes the same families. Yet there is little coordination between the two systems, and at times they may seem to be working at odds.

This chapter focuses on how the criminal justice and child welfare systems can work together more productively to support incarcerated parents and their children, whether those children are in kinship families or in formal out-of-home care through the child welfare agency. While other chapters of this handbook focus more directly on changes under the control of child welfare workers, this chapter looks at changes on the policy and program levels. It explores some of the challenges and opportunities in systemic collaboration, identifies systemic (i.e., policy and program) needs, and presents a range of examples of systemic responses.

Challenges and Opportunities in Systemic Response

Clearly, neither the criminal justice system nor the child welfare system intends to harm children, nor do they consciously ignore the needs of incarcerated parents and their children. Yet there is a failure to recognize this population or to coordinate treatment efforts, which has had negative effects on the children and families involved. There are several understandable reasons for this lack of effort.

- There are fundamental differences between the two systems. The purpose of the child welfare system is to ensure the safety, permanence, and well-being of children. It focuses on the child, but views the child as part of a family system that must be engaged to meet the child's needs. On the other hand, the purpose of the corrections system is to protect society from criminals, and the focus is on the prisoner as an individual rather than as a part of a family. These purposes may work at odds (e.g., providing visitations and working toward permanency may be threatened by prison policies geared toward security), and the potential benefit to each system by working collaboratively (i.e., supporting parenting enhances child safety, permanence, and well-being while also aiding in inmate rehabilitation) may go unappreciated.

Child welfare is dominated by and/or heavily influenced by the social work profession and only recently began to focus on more interdisciplinary approaches. On the other hand, while social workers and psychologists may work within the corrections system, it is dominated by criminal justice professionals. Each profession has its own values, philosophical approaches, theories, and methods, and sometimes these may appear incompatible, with staff seeing one another as adversaries rather than partners.

- Both systems are complex. Each system has many players (e.g., law enforcement officers, court personnel, correction officers and other staff, prison advocates, community-based service providers, CPS workers, licensing workers, treatment workers, family preservation workers) and a body of law, policies, rules, and practices that guide their work. It is a challenge for staff to understand relevant information about their own system, much less another system altogether.

- Both systems are overwhelmed. Prisons are overcrowded and the focus is on keeping order and maintaining security while housing too many inmates in too little space.

At the same time, child welfare agencies continue to reel from the events begun in 1974 with the passage of the Child Abuse Prevention and Treatment Act (CAPTA) (P.L. 93-247). When, as a result of that legislation, states began to mandate reporting of child abuse and neglect, the number of child maltreatment reports soared beyond any expectations, out-of-home placement was seen as the treatment of choice, and child welfare agencies entered a crisis mode from which they have yet to recover. Meanwhile, changing social conditions (e.g., drugs, HIV, increasing poverty) have exacerbated the problem.

Despite several legislative attempts to turn the system around (the Adoption Assistance and Child Welfare Act of 1980, P.L. 96-272; the Family Preservation and Support Services Act in 1993, P.L. 103-66; the Adoption and Safe Families Act of 1997, P.L. 105-89) and new approaches to intervention (e.g., specialized foster homes, dual track, family conferencing), child welfare has not been able to keep pace with need. The child welfare system, like the corrections system, has its hands full and, understandably, may not be eager to expand services (e.g., supportive services to kinship families) or grapple with new issues (e.g., permanency planning with incarcerated parents).

• There is a lack of data on common populations. While individual staff in either system might gather case-specific information, typically neither system includes such information on a data base. The criminal justice system doesn't know how many inmates are parents and the child welfare system doesn't know how many and which children in their caseloads have parents in prison. In addition, collecting data on children may be difficult, since children come into care at different times in relation to parental incarceration (e.g., at the time of arrest, at the time of sentencing, or during incarceration), and kinship families are difficult to track in the community.

In general, responses at a policy and program level are more likely to arise in response to systemically documented needs rather than from anecdotal information. If there is no systemic documentation and recognition of a particular situation, it is unlikely that policies and programs to address the problem will be forthcoming.

• There is insufficient knowledge on this population. Not only do we lack data concerning the numbers or characteristics of children and families that are affected, but we also lack research and practice wisdom or other information to guide us in serving this population. We have insufficient research on the impact of parental incarceration on children, the effectiveness of interventions, and the outcomes of various child caring arrangements.

As a result of these challenges, there are gaps in services to children and families that are evident from a family's first contact with the criminal justice system. A family's needs—needs of the child, the incarcerated parent, and the caregiver—may begin at the time an arrest is made and continue through the incarceration and the return of the parent to the community. The needs may include such things as information about where children are and how they are doing; support for visits between parents and children in care; support for the caregiving family; information regarding a range of criminal justice and child welfare processes; notification of hearing dates; and collaborative and appropriate decision-making and permanency planning.

While these challenges to developing systemic responses are formidable, there are compelling reasons for forging new collaborative arrangements between child welfare and corrections systems:

- Improved computer systems are capable of handling data differently. As agencies continue to upgrade data systems, the potential for collecting, storing, and sharing information to improve our understanding of service needs is improving.

- Current philosophies of service delivery emphasize such concepts as coordination and collaboration, breaking down agency barriers, interdisciplinary work, family-centered practice, service accessibility, and holistic approaches. Holistic approaches enable us to see more clearly the interconnectedness of a variety of family and community problems—poverty, crime, alcohol and substance abuse, and child protection—and the need for comprehensive interventions.

- Despite differing philosophies and practices, there are common goals between the two systems, and each can help the other to achieve these goals. Inmate rehabilitation involves helping them to effectively resume life roles, and to many inmates, parenting is one of the most important of these roles. At the same time, rehabilitation of parents to assume full-time care of their children or to continue or establish a life-long positive relationship with their children is critical to child safety, permanency, and well-being. Thus, collaboration is in the best interests of both systems and the families they serve.

- While the period of parental incarceration can present challenges to service providers, it may also be viewed as a good opportunity for intervention with families. For many parents, particularly mothers, prison can be a time when they get sober and can focus on their relationships with their children. As harsh as prison conditions may be, for some they are a respite from an even harsher and more chaotic life on the outside. During this time, parents may be more receptive to services, as the disruption in their lives leave them "destabilized" and thus open to change. Away from the demands of maintaining sobriety and functioning in chaotic environments, they may gather up the motivation to become better parents and to address a broad range of issues affecting family. Yet realizing the potential benefits depends upon both systems having policies and practices that are friendly to parental rehabilitation. For the child welfare worker, the parent is literally a "captive audience" and may be more accessible than he or she would be in the community.

- For children, the enforced separation from the parent, while disruptive and painful, presents opportunities as well as dangers. Children whose lives have been characterized by chaos may experience this period as a time of relative calm and stability. For all children, it is a time during which their needs can be focused on, and the caregiver can potentially assist the child with developmental strides. Yet again, realizing the benefits depends upon system collaboration.

Policy and Program Suggestions

The opportunity and benefits of responding systemically to the needs of incarcerated parents and their children inspire us to address the challenges. We might begin with the following suggestions:

- Establish better mechanisms for collecting, storing, and sharing information on incarcerated parents and their children. Systematically collecting information may include such strategies as mandating that certain information be elicited from clients of each system, establishing protocols for collecting information, and conducting agency-wide needs assessments. The data could be entered into agency data bases and made available in a variety of report formats for documenting the extent and nature of the problem and for case-by-case sharing of information.

- Develop cross-system ties between child welfare and criminal justice systems. This may begin with formal interagency task forces or study groups to identify common needs and policies and practices that are barriers to collaboration and family support. Interagency agreements may be established, delineating roles, responsibilities, resources, and communication processes for identifying and working with incarcerated parents and their children. Interagency staffing of cases can enhance appreciation of multiple systems' perspectives and help all focus on families' needs.

- Provide cross-systems training to help develop shared perspectives, enhance staff's understanding of the complexities of each system, and forge relationships among staff that will support ongoing collaborative work.

- Develop incarcerated parents and their children as an area of specialization and/or as a specialized function within each system. Because child welfare staff already feel overwhelmed, and because the percentage of their cases involving parental incarceration is not large, carving this out as an area of specialization may provide the necessary focus and expertise without further burdening staff. This may be accomplished through such mechanisms as specialized units, specialized workers, and specialized foster parents who understand and will support incarcerated parents and their children.

- Develop community-wide responses that can provide holistic interventions, from prearrest and preincarceration through aftercare. Given the interconnectedness of the endangering conditions that point families toward criminal activities and make the path to rehabilitation so difficult, a wide range of community-based agencies have services relevant to arrested and/or incarcerated parents and their children.

- Identify existing resources in the community and consider better ways of using those resources. For example, is there a way to work collaboratively with the informal and formal community-based support groups for ex-offenders and families of offenders? Could these organizations be used to provide some of the unique services needed by clients? Could these organizations be used to build alliances between the child welfare and criminal justice systems?

- Look specifically at how to meet the needs of the children. Sometimes when children and/or families become known to one system that focuses on a particular aspect of their lives (e.g., parental crime, retardation, mental health problems, learning disabilities), ambiguity and "jurisdictional disputes" result in unmet needs. Yet in the case of children with incarcerated parents, they will likely have a range of problems, including difficulties preceding the crime and arrest; trauma associated with criminal behavior, arrest, and incarceration; separation and loss issues; and unmet safety and stability needs. Thus, any interagency or community-wide planning must consider how to share responsibility for identifying and meeting the needs of these children, regardless of the system in which they or their parents first appear.

Examples of Systemic Responses

Despite the general lack of attention to the needs of incarcerated parents and their children, a few child welfare agencies have begun to engage in collaborative work with state and local departments of corrections. For example, one state agency provides local social services with a contact person at each correctional facility to coordinate visits and services. Another agency has assigned a social worker to a women's prison to act as a liaison for crises involving inmates' children. A third state agency assigns specialized staff to cases in which women give birth while incarcerated. In other creative collaborations, child welfare agencies have worked cooperatively with corrections officials to establish eligibility for community treatment programs, collaborated with community service providers to arrange counseling for families and special recreational activities for children, and collaborated with state prisons to establish special facilities for parent-child visitation [CWLA 1998].

A needs assessment initiated by the Maryland Department of Human Resources in 1996 provides one model for child welfare agencies wishing to collaborate with the criminal justice community. The initial project activities included collecting background information about parental incarceration in Maryland; convening a focus group of child welfare caseworkers and managers to discuss their experiences working with incarcerated parents and their children; visiting Maryland prisons and detention centers to understand how facilities, processes, and programs impact child welfare goals; and building more collaborative relationships between Maryland's child welfare and corrections officials [Conly 1998].

Chapter 5

Community Services to Support and Preserve Families

One goal of child welfare is to prevent children from coming into care by strengthening and supporting the family. Family support services are defined as an array of services—e.g., counseling, economic support, health/medical services, housing assistance—that enable a family to remain intact and provide for child safety, permanence, and well-being. Family support services may be offered to birth families, foster families, kinship care providers, or adoptive families. Family preservation services are defined as services offered to a family to avoid placement when there is a child specifically at risk of placement (the term is also sometimes used to refer to reunification services).

Regarding parental incarceration, we are primarily interested in family support and preservation in two situations: actually avoiding the mother's incarceration and a child's subsequent out-of-home placement by using community alternatives to incarceration, and maintaining a child's stability by supporting kinship care arrangements.

Alternatives to Incarceration

Because of the limited effectiveness of incarceration in achieving criminal justice system goals and the unintended consequences that are destructive to family and community life, there is much interest today in alternatives to incarceration.

Limited Effectiveness of Incarceration

What is the criminal justice system designed to achieve? Overall, the purpose is to protect society from lawbreakers. Theoretically, this is accomplished by meeting four goals to which one may attach various degrees of importance—incapacitation, retribution, deterrence, and rehabilitation.

Incapacitation refers to keeping criminals out of society so they cannot commit other crimes during the period of incarceration. Retribution is punishing those who break the law. Deterrence is based on the belief that inmates are less likely to commit future crimes if they are punished for their current crimes, and that other society members who witness the punishment are less likely to commit crimes. Rehabilitation involves changing the inmates, enabling them to deal more effectively with postincarceration life [Brooks and Bahna 1994].

Though incarceration does generally incapacitate and punish criminals, there is little evidence that this results in any long-term reduction in criminal activity. The extent to which incarceration achieves its other goals is questionable. For instance, in relation to deterrence, one might expect those most affected by a criminal's behavior, the children, to be deterred from crime, while in fact many studies have shown the opposite is true [Brooks and Bahna 1994]. In terms of rehabilitation, it is more likely that the experience of incarceration will desocialize inmates, teaching them to survive in the jail or prison but rendering them nonfunctional in society. While some prisons do have good rehabilitation programs, these programs must address not only the inmates' original problems, but also those created by the confinement.

Not only is it equivocal how well incarceration meets the intended goals, but incarceration also has some unfortunate unintended consequences. Separating lawbreakers from their families generally creates family upheaval for which children and society will bear the consequences. Because the inmate is unable to fulfill responsibilities to family, the family may suffer more than the inmate does, so retribution is visited upon the innocent. The disruption of family life not only increases the likelihood that the inmate's children will later commit crimes but also, according to some studies, increases the criminal behavior of the ex-inmate.

Given these concerns regarding the effects of incarceration, a larger cross-systems view of incarceration is called for. While the overall purpose of protecting society is important, we need to look for means that can accomplish that goal with minimal detrimental effects to children and families, thus protecting society today and in the future. Ideally, we would look toward options that impose only the amount of confinement and control that is necessary, while providing the opportunity for rehabilitation in as natural an environment as possible, given the need for security.

There is a trend today toward tougher sentencing guidelines, mandatory sentencing for certain crimes, and increasing numbers of incarcerated women. While courts may take family situations into account in sentencing, many are reluctant to do so. At the same time, however, interest in community-based alternatives is increasing. The expense of incarceration, serious overcrowding of facilities, and recognition of the cost to families have led many to look toward viable alternatives to incarceration.

Community Alternatives

Watson & McAninch [1997] examined the range of available alternatives to incarceration:

- **Probation and parole.** Both probation (imposed by a trial court judge) and parole (granted by a board of probation, parole, and pardon services) provide for the offender to serve a sentence in the community rather than through incarceration. Probation and parole are available only to certain offenders (related to such things as type of crime and recidivism). Each imposes certain conditions that may relate to, for example, employment, family support, reporting to an officer, and remaining crime- and substance-free. Probation and parole may also include community service, random drug testing, curfews, or surveillance. Unpaid work for private nonprofit or public organizations may also be imposed.

- **Home detention.** Low-risk, nonviolent criminals may be allowed to serve a sentence at home. (Drug offenders are frequently barred from these programs.) The detention may allow approved absences from home and may include electronic monitoring.

- **Fines, restitution, and forfeitures.** These alternatives are frequently used for property crimes as well as other misdemeanors and some felonies. A fine is paid to the court, while restitution is turned over to the crime victim. Sometimes restitution may be paid not to the victim, but to society through community service. Forfeiture involves giving up property connected with commission of a crime (e.g., a car used in the distribution of drugs). For the indigent, reasonable payment schedules are usually set up to avoid unequal accessibility of the alternatives.

- **Pretrial diversion.** This is a pretrial intervention that channels offenders to self-help or other treatment programs to avoid an arrest record and further involvement with the criminal justice system. Pretrial diversion is usually not available for violent crimes or serious drug offenses.

- **Partial incarceration.** Under this alternative, the offender may spend evenings and weekends incarcerated and weekdays in the community under supervision. The option may also include counseling, community work projects, and restitution.

- **Restitution centers and halfway houses.** A variety of community-based residential settings are being developed, in which offenders may continue most of their life roles while living in a supervised setting and perhaps paying off restitution. Some of these allow families to remain together, and they may focus specifically on treatment for substance abuse.

All of these alternatives impose varying degrees of restriction and accountability upon the criminal while allowing participation in family and community life. Thus, they may provide the ideal opportunity for working with a woman on the conditions that led to her criminal behavior and helping her establish or reestablish a viable family and community life. The criminal justice and child welfare systems could be mutually supportive, as improved functioning in life roles provides some buffer against future crime.

Examples of Programs

Examples of community-based female offenders' programs that can meet the needs of both the criminal justice and the child welfare systems are plentiful.

- **Crossroads.** Crossroads is "an intensive (five days/week, all day) out-patient program for female substance abusers facing felony charges" [Conly 1998, p. 23] or those charged with violations of parole or probation. The focus is on women who are pregnant or have small children, and mothers are allowed to bring children to the program site while they participate in the program.

- **DAMAS.** Daughters and Mothers Alternatives to Incarceration Services (ATI) provides a structured and supportive environment in a day treatment setting in which women's needs can be addressed through either in-house services or referral services. The program is available to women incarcerated for felony offenses in New York [Conly 1998].

- **Hopper Home Alternative to Incarceration Program.** Clients in this New York-based program begin with a period of residence at Hopper Home, during which they receive intensive supervision, case management services, and skill-building training, followed by assisted transition back into the community [Conly 1998].

- **ARC House/ARC Community Services, Inc.** This Wisconsin residential treatment program for women awaiting trial, sentenced to the program, or on parole allows gradual lifting of restrictions and reintegration into the community and provides services regarding a range of issues (substance use, abuse, criminality, health, employment, parenting, child custody, and reunification) [Bloom & Steinhart 1993].

- **Summit House.** Serving pregnant women, this community-based residential program in North Carolina provides structure, close supervision, therapeutic services including individual and group counseling, a Narcotics Anonymous program, and educational programs addressing such issues as parenting, health, family life, employment, and social skills [Bloom & Steinhart 1993].

- **Community Prisoner Mother Program.** These residential programs in California allow mothers and their young children to live together in small, structured, community-based facilities. Services to the mothers include occupational and life skills training, counseling, employment in the community, and child care. [Bloom & Steinhart 1993].

Not every offender can use community-based alternatives. Some, due to a record of violence and inability to control their antisocial behavior in the absence of strict confinement, are such a threat to society that they must be incarcerated. But for those who can use less restrictive alternatives, such programs offer promising approaches toward preserving and strengthening families to ensure minimal disruption to children and to their safety, permanency, and well-being.

Supporting Kinship Families

When mothers are incarcerated, their children often live with relatives, most often the maternal grandmother. In most situations, mothers themselves make decisions regarding a child's living arrangements, but the child welfare agency may become involved. Sometimes child welfare agencies are reluctant to offer family support services to relative caregivers, particularly if they were not involved in the placement and/or do not have custody of the child. There are good reasons for this reluctance. Child welfare agencies are already overloaded trying to meet their mandated responsibilities. In addition, many families would not welcome the intrusion of the agency into their lives.

Kinship families, however, despite their many strengths, may also have many unmet needs. For instance, taking on the incarcerated woman's child will most likely impose financial hardship, upset established family patterns and roles, involve the family with the criminal justice system, and challenge them to cope with a distressed child's behavior and find treatment resources.

If the agency is formally involved with the family or is able to arrange for services that the family will accept, many of these needs can be met through a range of community support services. The goal of such services is to strengthen and support kinship families and avert breakdown of the care arrangement. Many of these arrangements are fragile, and in the absence of supports, families may be unable to maintain the safe and stable homes that children require.

A later chapter of this guide will examine workers' direct services to kinship families (e.g., establishing guardianship, determining eligibility for financial and Medicaid services). Here are examples of some community-based programs for children of incarcerated parents and their caregivers.

- **Grandparents as Parents (GAP).** Increasingly grandparents find their plans for retirement and normal grandparenting interrupted when it becomes necessary for them to take responsibility for their grandchildren. While they love their grandchildren and want to help, many also experience anger, financial hardship, role overload, and stress-related health problems. GAP and similar programs offer support groups in which grandparents can share their feelings and discuss their issues with others having similar experiences. The groups may also offer educational programs, referrals, actual material resources, and respite care [Poe 1995].

- **Aid to Children of Imprisoned Mothers, Inc. (AIM).** Located in Atlanta, Georgia, AIM serves incarcerated mothers, their children, and family members. Services include provision of educational materials about dealing with the criminal justice system, transportation to prisons, children's services (e.g., summer camp, after-school tutoring), and caregiver-child support groups [Bloom & Steinhart 1993].

- **Chicago Legal Aid to Incarcerated Mothers, Inc. (CLAIM).** Serving incarcerated women, and their children and families in Illinois, CLAIM offers classes, support groups, and printed material addressing legal issues regarding parental rights, child custody, legal guardianship, kinship care, and visitation [Bloom & Steinhart 1993].

Practice Tips

While child welfare administrators and workers generally will not be directly involved in alternative sentencing and community-based programs such as those described in this chapter, the agency's interest in family preservation and support would suggest that staff need to be aware of these options and work with the criminal justice system and the community toward creating and using family-friendly, community-based services. Thus, child welfare staff should do the following:

- Be aware of the deleterious effects of incarceration on children and families.

- Research the available incarceration alternatives in your state and community, how and for whom they are used, and how you might advocate for their increased use.

- Be aware of the needs of kinship families who are providing care to these children.

- Find out what family support services for relatives of incarcerated women are available in your community, advocate for such services, and make appropriate referrals when you are serving such families.

Chapter 6

Practice Needs: Protecting Children when a Parent Is Arrested

Usually, the child welfare agency's involvement with an incarcerated parent's family will begin with child protective services (CPS), just as this is the "door" to agency involvement with most other families. In fact, because many of these families have led troubled lives characterized by poverty, substance involvement, and family and community violence, CPS may have already been involved with the family before the current crisis of arrest and incarceration.

Thus, there may have been an earlier CPS investigation, and the agency may even be offering in-home services to the family at the time a parent is arrested and subsequently incarcerated. This situation usually necessitates a new living arrangement for the child. An earlier CPS investigation may, on the other hand, have resulted in out-of-home care for a child. In this case, a parent's subsequent arrest and incarceration could mean that other children in the home would then need to be placed. In any event, it would certainly require a reassessment of the service plan and a new mode of working with the family to accommodate the arrest and incarceration.

This chapter will focus on what happens when a parent is arrested and CPS is not currently working with a family (though they may have been in the past). It describes first what might typically happen when a parent is arrested and the unpredictable events following the arrest. (Because of the great variation in how certain procedures may be carried out across different circumstances, no attempt is made here to be comprehensive. Rather, the intent is to present likely scenarios.) Next, it looks at what happens to the child during this initial period. This is followed by a discussion of caregiving arrangements, including how CPS might become involved. After a summary of issues, interventions, strategies, and practice tips are offered as mechanisms for improving the way both child welfare and criminal justice handle arrest and subsequent events.

What Happens to the Parent?

We have already seen that many of these children have lived with the constant trauma of poverty; exposure to ongoing drug use, violence, and other criminal behaviors; entanglements with the law; and unstable living arrangements. For these children, the arrest of a parent is neither the first nor an isolated event.

Whether the arrest of a parent is one more trauma in a chaotic family life or a new and unique trauma, it moves the family into a special kind of crisis. Involvement with the criminal justice system—beginning with arrest and sometimes leading to incarceration—starts a process that may be long, complicated, unfamiliar, and unpredictable. Particularly upon a first arrest, the process is largely a mystery, and there is usually nobody available to explain it. Not only the events themselves, but also the time lapses between events are unpredictable.

What might a parent typically experience when she is arrested and afterward? Here's a thumbnail sketch.

The Arrest and Booking

A mother may be arrested for a variety of misdemeanors or felonies—e.g., traffic violations, shoplifting, illegal drug possession, distributing drugs, fraud, or prostitution. The officer may have seen the crime being committed (e.g., traffic violation) or the crime may have been reported (e.g., shoplifting). If the officer witnessed the crime or has probable cause to believe the person committed a crime, he or she will make an arrest—especially if the crime is freshly committed—or, in some cases, issue a warrant.

It is likely that the arresting officer knows nothing about the woman or her circumstances—her children, employment, or other obligations. An important exception would be if the arrest is made by a narcotics officer, in which case the house will have been under surveillance and a great deal will be known about the woman and her family.

A search may or may not accompany the arrest. The officer may have a search warrant, allowing him/her to search a suspect's house, car, person, and immediate surroundings. Even without a warrant, an officer may search to seize evidence that might disappear, stop and frisk a person when illegal activity is suspected, or search a stopped vehicle. The officer may perform a pat down if there is any question that the suspect may be hiding weapons that could pose a danger to herself or others.

When the arrest is made, the woman's hands may be cuffed behind her back, especially if she is belligerent and the situation is volatile, but this is at the officer's discretion. She will be put into a paddy wagon or caged patrol car with doors that can only be opened from the outside and transported to a municipal or county jail or detention center, where an arrest warrant will be issued in the case of a warrantee's arrest, and the arrest will be booked. (If there is insufficient evidence at this time that this person committed a crime, no warrant will be issued, and she will be released.) Booking involves entering the person's name, criminal charge, other relevant facts, and possibly photographing and fingerprinting. After booking, some interrogation typically follows. If the woman is to be placed in a holding cell, all her property will be taken from her, inventoried, and secured, and any items with which she might harm herself, such as shoelaces or belts, will be removed. She may also have to give up her clothes and change into a uniform. The process from arrest to a holding cell will typically take about two hours, depending upon person-power and space availability.

Hearings

Usually within 24–48 hours, the arrestee will make an initial appearance before a judge, who will decide whether there is probable cause to detain her, and whether or not she may be released pending further hearings if probable cause if found. Pretrial release has tremendous advantages, allowing the accused to return to family and employment, and work with a lawyer on a defense. If granted, the arrestee may be released on her own recognizance, or bail may be required. The arrestee may be released to the custody of another person or organization and restrictions such as drug tests may be imposed. If the person is deemed dangerous or a poor risk for returning for trial, the bail request will be denied and the person detained.

At some point, an arrestee may be diverted from trial through a mechanism called pretrial diversion, negotiated between lawyers. This is a cost-efficient option in cases in which there is little criminal history, the current crime did not involve violence, the arrestee poses no threat to the community, and her needs would be better met outside the criminal justice system. Typically, she would see a counselor, perform volunteer service, use special treatment (such as drug and alcohol treatment, vocational rehabilitation, or mental health services), and perhaps pay some form of restitution. If this option is not offered and accepted, the process usually proceeds to a preliminary hearing.

At a preliminary hearing, the judge determines whether there is probable cause to believe the accused committed a crime. If probable cause if found, the case may be presented to a grand jury for consideration and possible indictment. Other cases may proceed by the issuance of formal charges, sometimes called an information, submitted by the prosecutor. Once charges are filed, the accused is scheduled for arraignment at which she is asked to enter a plea. If she pleads guilty and the plea is accepted, she gives up the right to a trial and may be sentenced at that time. If she pleads not guilty, she proceeds to trial. A "not guilty" verdict at trial ends the process, and the she will be free of any further involvement with the justice system on the suspected crime.

If she is found guilty, she will be held for a sentencing hearing; the sentence may include restitution, fines, probation, incarceration, or death. It may also be a suspended sentence or a sentence to suitable community service. A defendant may then decide to appeal her conviction or sentence by asking an appellate court to review the case.

The timing of these events is uncertain. Depending upon the docket and availability of a judge, anywhere from a few days to over a month may elapse between hearings. Several months could be involved if the case is to go to trial, particularly a jury trial. In addition, there clearly is considerable room for discretion within this process. This is a good thing, as it gives local law enforcement, magistrates, and judges some flexibility in responding to various circumstances—nature of the offense, history of offending, and other special circumstances. On the other hand, the discretion contributes to the uncertainty of the process for mother and family.

Impact on Parent

For the parent, this lack of knowledge and uncertainty creates a sense of loss of control, confusion, and anxiety. Whatever routines or plans she may have had for that day, that week, or sometime into the future are disrupted, and she can't predict in what ways or for how long.

The parent may also experience considerable embarrassment and shame, as she is cuffed, escorted by one or more uniformed officers to a patrol car, and driven away. This may occur in a store or on the street, where acquaintances and strangers may gawk, or it may occur at home, with curious neighbors looking on. Particularly if the parent is under the influence of substances at the time of the arrest, there may be a struggle that adds to the confusion and may require more assertive action by the officers, thus creating more of a "scene."

What Happens to the Child?

The Arrest

If a child of the parent is present at the time of the arrest, the child witnesses the forced removal of the parent, as well as the parents' confusion, embarrassment, and shame. The parent will feel a loss of credibility in the child's eyes. It is important to remember that, regardless of what a parent has done, the child needs to see the parent as powerful and in charge. Yet when a child witnesses a parent's arrest, he or she sees the parent being disempowered, leaving the child feeling exposed and vulnerable. Thus, the child's immediate reactions my include feelings of helplessness, bitterness about the way the parent was arrested, and anger toward the arresting officers. The reaction may be especially strong if the parent resists arrest and the officers have to use force. Besides the immediate trauma, witnessing the arrest may influence how the child later views police and law enforcement—as intrusive and abusive rather than protective, as is their true purpose. It has been estimated that 20% of children with incarcerated mothers witnessed their mother's arrest [Johnston 1995a].

If the child doesn't witness the arrest, someone else has to tell the child that his or her mother has been arrested and that it is uncertain when she will return. While the child is saved from the trauma of witnessing the arrest, he or she will have a dimmer view of the reality of the event, and whatever isn't carefully explained, the child will fill in with fantasy—abandonment, abduction, permanent separation—that may be even worse than the reality.

Immediately After the Arrest

If the child is with the parent at the time of the arrest, he or she will probably be separated from the parent and handed over to another officer, who will transport the child to police headquarters or to the jail or detention center. The child will be kept there while the parent is being processed and until care arrangements can be made. Some officers will allow time for the mother to tell her child good-bye, and some keep toys in the trunks of their cars in the event that they will transport children. However, officers may have had no formal training in responding to or communicating with children and may not be sensitive to children's needs.

During this waiting period, the treatment of the child may depend wholly upon the officers' sensitivity. Though a department may or may not have clear procedures around handling of children, many officers are parents themselves and will go out of their way to make the child comfortable. A secretary, officer, or victim advocate may sit with the child. If the arrest was at home and the arresting officer was especially attuned to the child's feelings, the officer may even have allowed the child to take a personal belonging (teddy bear, doll, book, or toy truck) from home. The sensitive officer will understand the child's need for information—about what will happen to the child, what is happening with the parent, how long it will last, and when the child will see the parent again—and will provide it at an age-appropriate level. However, given the uncertainty of the process, it may be impossible to adequately reassure the child.

If a child is not present when the parent is arrested, the arresting officer may or may not ask about children. However, if the officer is made aware of children, he or she will usually follow up. A child may be at school, in which case the officer should contact the school. There, a school official, such as principal or guidance counselor, will talk with the child, sometimes jointly with the law enforcement officer, to explain what has happened. Also, the school records should show the names of responsible relatives and provide other helpful information about the child and family. Some schools now have law enforcement officers (school resource officers) assigned to them. Such an officer, already known to the children and seen in a positive light, would be the ideal person to help the child understand what was happening.

Sometimes the child may not be present and the parent may not know where he or she is. Some officers will go out of their way to ask neighbors and relatives or check out places that children might hang out.

Practice around the involvement of CPS varies. Sometimes law enforcement procedures include calling CPS at the time of the arrest, particularly if the arrest was due to any form of child maltreatment. In this case, CPS would take the child from the site, perhaps in an unmarked vehicle. In other situations, CPS may be called to pick up the child either from the police station or from school. Of course, many times CPS is not called at all.

Finding a Caregiver

Though this does not necessarily happen, it is best if, either at the time of the arrest or soon thereafter, the officer asks the parent her preferences for child care arrangements and honors these wishes if possible. Occasionally, CPS or another agency will conduct a home study of the proposed caregiver's home to determine its suitability. This may involve an on-site inspection of the home and a criminal records check. If the mother cannot name a caregiver (no one is available or she is incapable of deciding because of alcohol or drugs) CPS will be called in to find a suitable placement. It is possible that CPS, like law enforcement, has no specific policies for responding to arrests, so its involvement may depend upon individual workers' sensitivity, ingenuity, and relationship with law enforcement.

Whether the mother will be allowed to make child care arrangements or to handle other "loose ends," such as notifying an employer, will depend on the flexibility of the individual police department. She may be given freedom to make calls or may designate someone else to make calls for her. On the other hand, she may have little access to a telephone and little help as she tries to locate and engage a caregiver—with no preparation and often few resources—to assume responsibility for her child and assist with other tasks [Katz 1998].

Even when best practice is followed, this series of events is traumatic for parent and child. When best or even adequate practice is not followed, the consequences for the child can be devastating. If there is not an available caretaker and CPS isn't called, children are sometimes placed in community shelters or in nonsecure units at juvenile detention facilities. For these children, the trauma of separation may be compounded by fear for their own safety and assault to their self-esteem.

When Caregiving Arrangements Break Down

Sometimes CPS becomes involved when a parent's arrangement for the child breaks down or the child's safety is in jeopardy. The child might have experienced tremendous instability, perhaps having been passed from relative to relative until either the current caregiver, the mother herself, or a third party calls CPS. In addition, because caregivers may be unable to handle an entire sibling group, brothers and sisters may be separated from one another. Thus, by the time CPS is notified, the child's trauma may be a complex mix of maltreatment, an endangering home situation, separation from siblings, and/or multiple moves.

Meanwhile, the mother may be feeling increasingly frustrated at her inability to manage her children from afar, and relatives may feel increasingly put out with the responsibilities being thrust upon them.

Feeling understandably frustrated, the mother may have a strong desire to play a more active and effective role in arranging adequate care for her children. She may also want to work on her transition back to her roles as caregiver and provider—positive steps for both mother and children. Yet the jail may not support her in her desires. Jails are designed for short-term stays. They are often overcrowded, have limited space, and give top priority to security. They are less likely than prisons to have special emphasis on parenting concerns, making it unlikely that they will have any sort of program to support parenting or to help the mother with her transitional needs upon release [Smith & Elstein 1994].

Summary of Issues

The above discussion has highlighted a number of issues of which the CPS worker must be aware:

- These children may be experiencing ongoing trauma and chaotic lives, possibly including prior maltreatment.

- The arrest and subsequent events involve additional trauma for child and parent.

- There is flexibility and variation in the processes through which the parent will proceed, and timelines are uncertain.

- The uncertainty raises anxiety levels, makes it difficult to give the child accurate information, and hampers the parent's ability to plan.

- Law enforcement policies and procedures regarding arrestees' children may be nonexistent or extensive, but in any case, the sensitivity of officers is a critical factor.

- Practices vary concerning when and whether CPS will be notified—at the scene, after the child has been transported, when a home check is needed, or when a living arrangement breaks down.

- Considering the sea of events before, during, and after arrest, CPS workers should always be screening for child maltreatment to identify those children either already suffering maltreatment or at risk due to the arrest and incarceration.

- Because of the prevalence of substance involvement of arrested women, CPS workers should screen particularly for this.

- The incarcerated parent who wants to be involved in planning for a child's care may receive little assistance and may face obstacles such as limited use of the telephone. She might be worried about what will happen if CPS becomes involved.

- Jails generally do not offer rehabilitation services to assist the mother with resumption of her caregiving and other life roles.

Interventions, Strategies, and Practice Tips

It is important to remember that neither the arrest, a finding of "guilty," nor subsequent incarceration removes from the parent her right and responsibility to provide for her children. Thus, any suggested approaches or services are meant to support, not supplant the mother's caregiving role, while ensuring child safety and protection.

Nationwide, practices regarding the handling of children and parental concerns upon the arrest of a parent vary widely. Fortunately, policies, practices, and programs that are sensitive to children's needs and parents' concerns suggest some helpful approaches.

The range of suggestions offered here covers system responses as well as specific improvements that are under the direct control of law enforcement officers and CPS workers.

- Establish interagency collaborative agreements and other links among law enforcement, CPS, schools, and community agencies that delineate roles and support ongoing working relationships.

- Establish protocols for law enforcement that cover various functions, including:
  — inquiring about any children and the provisions for their care at the time of the parent's arrest;
  — initial screening regarding child safety;
  — establishing availability of a suitable caregiver;
  — screening a caregiver's home (with or without CPS involvement), including on-site inspection and interviewing, criminal records check, and CPS records check;
  — documenting the child's living arrangement;
  — contacting CPS when child safety or lack of a caregiver is at issue.

- Expand the CPS mandate to cover services for these children, which would include:
  — interviewing children;
  — screening for child abuse and neglect initially and at any point there is concern;
  — screening for CPS involvement;
  — assessing suitability of potential caregiver;
  — finding a placement if necessary;
  — serving as consultants to law enforcement.

- Provide training for law enforcement, CPS, schools, and community agencies to improve the response when a child's parent is arrested and/or incarcerated. Joint training offers the opportunity for trainees to practice responding jointly and to forge personal relationships that will facilitate effective collaboration. Training should cover:
  — agency roles, whether established by law or interagency agreement;
  — agency protocols;
  — legal rights of parents;
  — possible reactions (emotional and behavioral) of both parents and children to the incarceration;

— informational and emotional needs of children, parents, and caregivers;

— good practice that supports a positive parent-child relationship and child safety;

— effective communicaton with children in an age-appropriate manner;

— situations in which children would need additional help.

• Identify special units, officers, and/or victim advocates to develop expertise in responding to children and their arrested parent.

• Ensure 24-hour availability of CPS personnel or liaison to respond rapidly and competently when called upon by law enforcement for assistance.

• Provide the parents with answers to the following questions in an understandable format:

— What will or might happen as their cases are processed?

— What are their legal rights and responsibilities (including custody issues and what may happen with her children) and what are the children's legal rights?

— How can they make arrangements for children's care?

— How can they remain an active parent in relation to such things as the child's education and extracurricular activities?

— What can they do if they have concerns that their children are not being taken care of properly by the caregiver?

• Allow a 72-hour protective custody hold for officers or CPS to work with the mother regarding care arrangements without having to go to court.

• Create child-friendly practices and environments for children awaiting placement, such as:

— allowing mothers to say good-bye to their children;

— allowing children to take a favorite toy with them;

— carrying toys in law enforcement vehicles, ready to give to children;

— ensuring a protected place for children to sit, providing toys at the station, and having a child-sensitive person sit with the child;

— allowing for early and extended parent-child visits;

— allowing contact visits (rather than through Plexiglas or wire mesh) when consistent with security;

— allowing child-sensitive, unobtrusive pat-down and search procedures, putting the burden for ensuring security on the parent rather than the child.

- Increase awareness among criminal court judges regarding needs of children with incarcerated parents, including:

  — impact of parent's absence on family structure;

  — impact on child of separation from parent and lack of contact;

  — impact of visitation and affect of geographical proximity.

- Have a range of emergency and short-term placements available that are specifically competent to deal with children whose parents have been arrested, including emergency foster homes and 24-hour shelter space for children of arrestees. Shelter space is especially critical for adolescents, whom other caregivers may be more hesitant to take.

- Provide caregivers information about:

  — what may happen as the parent proceeds through the criminal justice system;

  — what their responsibilities and authority are regarding the child's general care, health care, school, counseling, and other issues;

  — where to get support or help if they need it; and

  — what to do if they can no longer look after the child.

- Consider providing crisis and/or short-term intervention programs for parents at the jail to help them through the trauma of arrest, the legal process, and reentry adjustment.

- Identify community agencies that can provide follow-up in the community to allow transition from jail programs to community-operated support services.

- Delineate responsibilities and procedures for follow-up after placement to check on child safety and possible service needs.

Chapter 7

Practice Needs: Temporary Care in Out-of-Home Placement

The purpose of out-of-home placement is to provide temporary protection and nurturance for the child while preparing both child and parent for reunification or another permanent arrangement. The fact of a parent's incarceration does not alter these purposes. The practice issues associated with out-of-home placement in general are also applicable if a parent is incarcerated. The incarceration adds a new dimension, however, calling for heightened sensitivity to a range of issues and additional practice considerations.

As stated previously, we don't have extensive data indicating how or why children with incarcerated parents come into care. Likewise, it is unclear the extent to which the problems experienced by children in care are attributable to family socioeconomic factors, parenting issues, or problems surrounding the incarceration itself. We do know that the most frequent care arrangement for children of incarcerated mothers is with a relative [Beckerman 1998; Bloom & Steinhart 1993]. Usually, the arrangement will be informal, and the child's grandmother or another relative will provide the needed care without the involvement of child welfare. If, however, a child is already in care, the parent cannot arrange care, or an informal arrangement breaks down, child welfare services become involved and places the child into formal kinship care or foster care. Less frequently, the child may be placed in group care because of special care and treatment needs or for other reasons.

Despite the limitations in our knowledge, we have identified some of the issues these families face and can apply our general practice knowledge and emerging specific practice wisdom to frame approaches to working with such families. It is clear that there are many variables in relation to each family's situation—i.e., age of child, gender, reason for placement, care arrangement—and each of these variables brings special issues. However, there are also numerous common issues.

This chapter will first examine some of the basic issues and challenges around case management, the importance of maintaining family contact, and strategies for supporting contact and continuing ties. Second, it will look at some special treatment needs and services for the incarcerated parent and her child. Third, it will examine special needs of caregivers, including kinship foster families and nonkinship foster families. Finally, interventions, suggestions, and practice tips are provided.

This chapter does not assume that the child welfare agency has special policies or programs focused on parental incarceration. While the issues raised and suggestions offered here are significant whether or not there is an agency-wide focus on the population, the existence of special-focused policies and programs will do much to support workers' ability to apply this information and to practice effectively with incarcerated mothers and their children.

Basic Issues and Challenges

Case Management

For the most part, caseworkers themselves are unprepared for entering the world of the corrections system and for providing the help that children and families need as they enter that system. Under the best of circumstances, dealing with the incarceration of a family member is challenging; but when it also involves placement of children, the difficulties are compounded. Conversely, we know well the hardship that a child's out-of-home care places upon families, and these difficulties are also compounded when the absent parent is incarcerated.

To effectively assist such families, the caseworker must (a) recognize and deal with his or her own feelings about crime, incarceration, and the institutional setting; (b) increase his or her knowledge about the criminal justice system, including people as well as policies and procedures; and (c) establish workable strategies for carrying out case management duties within that environment.

Worker's Feelings

Child welfare workers are experienced in dealing with the most horrendous acts against children, and while they never lose their sensitivity to these acts, chances are they do establish an internal mechanism for handling their feelings. However, because workers have less experience with other crimes, their feelings and reactions cannot be taken for granted. Some may see crimes such as murder and drug trafficking as less upsetting than child maltreatment, whereas others may have particularly negative reactions. The worker's honest critique of his or her own reactions is the best strategy for ensuring that negative feelings aren't unintentionally communicated to the child, making it more difficult for the child to maintain a positive view of the parent.

It is likely that the worker will have reactions to the prison setting. The physical structure of the prison combined with prison security procedures and armed security personnel create a strict and intimidating environment. Thus, it is important for the worker to visit the prison at least once to become familiar with procedures before taking a child on a visit. This will ensure a more controlled emotional reaction and will provide time for the worker to think ahead about how to explain the setting and its procedures to the child.

Because a high percentage of incarcerated parents, particularly mothers, have substance abuse issues, workers should also recognize and evaluate their feelings about addiction and their beliefs about an addict's ability to recover.

Worker's Knowledge of the Criminal Justice System

Upon contact with the criminal justice system, the worker is entering a world of rules and roles that are unfamiliar. Thus, to effectively carry out case management responsibilities, the worker needs to know how the criminal justice system operates—roles of various prison officials, policies that would affect working with the incarcerated parent and visiting, service availability, and how decisions affecting the parent are made. Despite any difficulties the incarceration might impose, the worker still carries the responsibility for working with the parent on an individualized, realistic, and effective case plan, communicating with the parent regularly on such things as court hearings and where the children are placed, and encouraging the parent's participation in making decisions about the child [Beckerman 1998; Bloom and Steinhart 1993]. Thus, the worker needs to develop strategies for effectively carrying out case management within the prison environment.

Case Management Strategies

The first and foremost strategies should be getting to know roles of various prison officials and establishing personal relationships with them as appropriate [Seymour 1998]. If there is a prison social work service, a social worker may be the primary point of contact and may serve as a guide through the corrections system, but the worker also may want to know other prison employees, depending upon the need. For instance, with whom must one communicate to arrange visits? Who has the authority to provide special exceptions to improve visitation conditions? Who might be a friendly face to offset the intimidation of visits? The worker's personal relationships with such people could spell the difference between being unable to arrange contact of any sort and being able to arrange visits that are family-friendly.

If relationships are effectively established, the worker can use these to learn about rules and regulations—and in a prison setting, most activities are highly regulated. These will include regulations around visiting hours, conditions, and telephone calls [Beckerman 1998]. For instance, sometimes prisoners cannot accept incoming calls, and outgoing calls must be made collect. This could be a difficult issue for workers because agencies often don't allow collect calls [Beckerman 1998].

Importance of Family Relationships

Regardless of the circumstances around child placement, a primary concern is maintenance (or sometimes reestablishment) of positive family relationships. We know that maintenance of family relationships is essential to successful reunification. Time apart, lack of information and misinformation, and poorly understood and poorly handled reactions of child and parent to the separation can erode relationships, depriving parent and child of something that is essential to both. Even when the case plan is an arrangement other than a return home, a positive parent-child relationship will benefit both parent and child throughout life.

Yet maintaining a positive relationship between an incarcerated parent and a placed child is fraught with difficulty. These center around (a) the child's view of the incarcerated parent and ability to understand the incarceration; (b) the temporary caregivers' view of the incarcerated parent; (c) visitation; and (d) other forms of communication.

Child's View of the Parent

Regardless of what a parent has done, it is important that a child feel loved rather than abandoned or rejected and that the child see positive attributes in the parent. There is no need to be unrealistic. The prior parent-child relationship might not have been good, yet illegal activity and imprisonment do not necessarily equate with bad parenting or a poor parent-child relationship in the eyes of the parent or the child [Hairston 1998]. In fact, the relationship might have been very good, the attachment strong, and the involuntary separation very painful to both parent and child.

Children need to know that their parent did not voluntarily abandon them and that they are missed by the parent. Children need not only to hear this, but also to experience it. In other words, the parent needs to demonstrate continued attachment to the child through concrete behaviors.

There are significant obstacles to this, which will be discussed further. The worker, while seeking to overcome these obstacles, must help the parent to understand the importance of her behavior to the well-being of the child. Likewise, the worker must help the child understand why the parent might not be able to demonstrate her love and concern as she might wish.

Knowing that the parent has committed a crime will create negative feelings in the child, either because of his or her own knowledge of right and wrong or because disapproval is communicated by others. If the child has been abused or neglected, he or she is already having to deal with ideas such as "good people do bad things," "Mother has a problem that she is working on," and "despite these problems, there are things to be proud of." This ability to accept and integrate the good and the bad requires fairly sophisticated thinking that even many adults find difficult. For the child of the incarcerated parent, the task is complicated by the facts of the crime. If the child is told enough to understand the crime, he or she may also experience disbelief, denial, shame, anger, and betrayal. In addition, the reactions of relatives, substitute caregivers, and other authority figures (e.g., teachers, clergy, neighbors) may influence how the child views the parent. If the crime was reported in the media, the child also has to deal with the blatant public nature of what was heretofore his or her private family life.

It is particularly difficult for a child to maintain a positive view of the parent when the crime and incarceration are shrouded in secrecy. Often family members maintain a conspiracy of silence, out of fear that the child will be tainted by the information or will follow in the parent's footsteps [Beckerman 1998, Kampfner 1995]. Yet the absence of age-appropriate information leaves room for fantasy to fill in the gaps, and while the fantasy may include positive stories about the parent, it will not be reality-based and will not lead to a healthy adjustment.

Normally when a child enters out-of-home care, the worker helps him or her to create a cover story—an acceptable way to explain their living arrangement to those who may inquire. The story should not be dishonest but should supply enough information to satisfy others without giving information that, for the child, is private, allowing the child to maintain self-esteem. Children learn to say something like, "I'm staying with the Tolivers for a few months while my mother works out some things." Creating the story is complicated when the parent is incarcerated, particularly if this is publicly known. But the purpose is still the same. The story helps the child avoid public humiliation and successfully negotiate a difficult social situation. The cover story may also reduce the child's negative experiences associated with the parent's incarceration, thereby increasing the odds that the child will be able to view the parent in a positive light.

Temporary Caregivers' View of the Incarcerated Parent

The temporary caregivers' view of the incarcerated parent greatly influences the ongoing relationship between parent and child. Every day, in subtle and overt ways, the caregiver sends messages to the child about the parent that may influence how the child views the parent. When the parent has maltreated the child, the caregiver might openly criticize the parent, making reference to what the parent did or how they damaged the child. Or the criticism may be more couched in implied comparisons—"We wouldn't let you be hungry (as your mother did)" or "We would never leave you alone at night (as your mother did)." While such references seem innocuous and may be offered to help the child feel more secure, they may instead lead the child to doubt his/her parents. It is best to offer supportive comments in a way that is less apt to be construed as criticism of the parent, for instance, "Lots of families are different, but at our house, we eat dinner together every night."

When a parent has committed a crime, the substitute caregiver may feel more negatively toward the parent. If the caregiver is a relative, the crime may be seen as bringing shame on the entire family, and the response may be secrecy or ostracizing the offending parent, either of which negatively influences the child's view of and relationship with the parent. The family may also have "family stories" that the incarceration becomes part of, and family stories often carry implied predictions—"Yeah, that side of the family turned out bad. . . ."

The temporary caregivers' view of the parent is important also because it will influence the extent and quality of ongoing contact between parent and child. If the caregivers' view is that the parent is "bad" and will negatively influence the child, the caregiver can add to the already formidable obstacles to parent-child contact. It is important to realize that caregivers are usually well-intended, and what we recognize as negative messages may be honest attempts to protect the child.

Agencies must provide caregivers with information and training on how their words and attitudes toward the parent affect the child.

Strategies for Supporting Family Relationships

A range of strategies to support family relationships during the period of a mother's incarceration is available to workers, yet there may be obstacles to implementing the strategies.

Visitation. Visitation is perhaps the most important mechanism for maintaining a positive parent-child relationship. Visits dispel fears, support attachment, and can even provide the opportunity for improving relationships. Without visits, memories fade or are replaced with fantasy [Hairston

1998]. It is well documented that lack of visitation is correlated with reduced probability of successful reunification [Hess & Proch 1993]. Given the importance of the parenting role to most female inmates, we may conjecture that continuing contact with children and participating in parenting helps maintain the inmates' self-esteem and thus contributes positively to her rehabilitation.

Despite this, approximately one-half of incarcerated parents receive no visits from their children, and others receive only infrequent visits [Snell & Morton 1994]. One reason is that, though they are highly desirable, visits are also problematic. Even when incarceration is not an issue, workers and families struggle with problems relating to logistics and conflicting emotions surrounding visits. These issues are even more complicated when a parent is incarcerated. Obstacles working against visitation include the following:

- **Distance.** While good practice dictates that out-of-home placements be near the parent(s) to facilitate visitation, the incarceration of a parent usually means considerable distance, since prisons are located centrally to serve a large geographical area. In addition, because there are fewer women prisoners than men, women's prisons are apt to be fewer in number and consequently farther away from the inmate's children. This makes visits more difficult. Families may have to dedicate a whole day to travel the distance, reducing the frequency of visits. In addition, for many families the cost is an issue. For workers pressed with other duties, sacrificing a whole day primarily for travel may be a demotivator.

- **Hours and scheduling.** If visitation is scheduled during regular working hours, caregivers may have trouble getting there; if it is outside regular working hours, the worker may have difficulty visiting. In addition, scheduling procedures may be cumbersome or poorly understood, resulting in delays. Even when visits are carefully arranged and caregivers arrive at the prison with children in tow, there may have been some disruption or security concern at the prison that results in the cancellation of all visits that day.

  Arranging for visits when siblings are involved presents other challenges. If siblings are living with different caregivers, coordinating transportation can be difficult. On occasion, the court may allow visits with one child but not another. It can also be hard for one caregiver or worker to manage several children—particularly younger children or children of different ages—during the often lengthy trip to the prison and through the prison security process.

- **Accommodations.** Even approaching a prison may be intimidating if security mechanisms, such as wire fencing and guard towers, are visible. Women may be housed in facilities that are somewhat less intimidating than those in which men are housed, but the facility will still have a somber, institutional look. The atmosphere inside is often inhospitable to children. There are usually no separate waiting rooms for children, and most rooms are not equipped with toys or other child-friendly decorations that would facilitate more natural parent-child contact. Visits might be confined to cubicles that lack privacy, or contact may be allowed only through glass or wire mesh barriers. In addition, facilities may be dirty, noisy, and overheated [Hairston 1998]. These settings are rarely conducive to the expression of real emotions, either positive or negative, or the discussion of important personal issues [Seymour 1998; Bloom 1995].

- **Procedures and requirements.** Prisons will have procedures and requirements, often connected with security, that may be uncomfortable or humiliating. A prolonged process of clearing may precede visits that last less than one-half hour. There may also be pat and frisk searches and rude treatment [Hairston 1998], since "outsiders" may be seen as unwelcome guests or intruders inside the prison, and any contact between outsiders and prisoners poses serious threats to security [Hairston 1998; Katz 1998]. Security precautions, geared to an occasional inmate who will try to sneak in contraband (possibly even in a child's diaper), may appear totally unreasonable and offensive to children, substitute caregivers, and workers who are there only to support the parent-child relationship. Negotiating these security processes—even in minimum security facilities—can heighten feelings of anxiety and may even be frightening for children.

- **Appearance and behavior of parent.** Sometimes the appearance and behavior of the parent may seem strange and frightening to the child, particularly during the first visit. The parent may be in prison garb or other clothing the child doesn't recognize. She may not have the same hairstyle or makeup, either because of not having access to the same beauty aides or lack of motivation. In addition, her behavior may be different because of her shame over the crime and incarceration, discomfort with seeing the child in that setting, or discomfort with the poor accommodations for the visit. These differences, strange to the child, may create an even greater feeling of distance in the parent-child relationship.

- **Jails.** While jails are generally closer to home than prisons, they may be even less child-friendly. Unlike prisons, jails almost universally require that visits be noncontact, with communication restricted to use of a phone through glass or mesh [Katz 1998]. In addition, because the anticipated stay is shorter, they are less apt to be attuned to child/parent relationship needs or to have special programs that support parenting.

- **Emotional components.** All these factors contribute to a flood of complex emotions poorly understood by parent, child, caregiver, and perhaps worker. As a result, sometimes parents don't want children to visit and children themselves are tentative about the visit, while caregivers and workers may point to the unpleasant emotions as a reason to postpone or discontinue visits [Hairston 1991, cited in Beckerman 1998].

Other Forms of Communication. While visitation is the primary and preferred means for maintaining contact and positive relationships between incarcerated parents and their children, the difficulties associated with visitation make it important to supplement visits with other forms of communication such as telephone calls and letters. However, there are also obstacles associated with these methods.

Prisoners do not have free and unfettered access to telephones. While the facility will contain pay phones, special arrangements may be required for using them. In addition, calls are expensive. Telephone companies may charge rates above those normally charged. In addition, long distance calls must be made collect, and caregivers may be unable or unwilling to accept charges. [Hairston 1998]. Letters can be a good option, depending upon literacy levels [Seymour 1998; Snell & Morton 1994]. However, outgoing letters may have been stamped with warnings that they are from a correctional facility, and the child or caregiver may find this upsetting. [Hairston 1998].

Each family might also design other creative ways to support the relationship. For instance, the mother may tape record messages or readings from a child's favorite books, or the caregivers might send pictures of the child enjoying everyday activities. Whatever forms of communication can be found (and are allowed) to maintain and support a positive parent-child relationship, to keep the reality of one another alive, will help with permanency planning and reducing trauma to the child.

Special Treatment Needs and Services

Visitation and other forms of family communication in themselves may be considered a primary component of treatment for all families experiencing out-of-home placement of a child. Regardless of what other services families may need or whatever the case goal, they all need support in building, rebuilding, and maintaining positive relationships. In this sense, families can be considered their own best service providers, but they often can't perform that function without help. Often trust has been shattered, boundaries breached, loyalties compromised, and relationships damaged. Anything the worker can do to address the obstacles and to further positive communication among all family members is considered treatment.

Another ubiquitous component of treatment is the worker's preparation and monitoring of the case plan. This, too, presents unique challenges. Everything said above about caregiver visits—the difficulties of establishing contact and maintaining relationships, learning prison policies, regulations, and routines—also applies to case worker visits, yet effective case planning and monitoring requires overcoming the obstacles. Preparing the case plan is also complicated by uncertainty about the length of the parent's sentence, particularly in the face of new federal and state legislation that shortens timeframes for achieving goals. This issue will be discussed in the next chapter.

Regardless of the case goal, the worker needs to supply information to the incarcerated parent on an ongoing basis—information about the children, such as where they are and how they are doing; about what is happening in terms of court hearings and case reviews; and about the parent's progress. The worker also needs to support parental participation in hearings and reviews. In some cases, arrangements can be made for a parent to attend a court hearing related to her child if the prison or jail receives sufficient notice of the hearing and transportation can be scheduled. When an incarcerated parent is unable to attend a hearing, she should be given information about the hearing and encouraged to participate via correspondence so as to retain a sense of involvement in the child's life.

Incarcerated parents and their children may need other services beyond those the worker can provide. While still the exception rather than the rule, many innovative programs designed to help preserve and extend an incarcerated woman's ability to parent and to help her child are now being offered. These may involve the woman only, the woman and her child, or it may include caregivers. Some are sponsored by the correctional institutions in which they operate, while others are sponsored by community groups and brought into the institution.

Services to the Parent and Child

Normally, when children are in care, federal law requires that "reasonable efforts" are made to reunify those children with their families. This means that parents must receive appropriate services geared toward correcting whatever parenting difficulties necessitated the placement. When a parent is incarcerated, this same requirement applies. Yet, in the prison context, such services may be very limited. However, examples of good programs do exist, though there may be obstacles to accessing them, and the worker may want to ask about such programs and advocate for them should they not already be available.

Service Availability

Usually, when planning services for parents whose children are in care, the child welfare worker will consider what is available in the community, some communities being resource-rich and others resource-poor. When a parent is incarcerated, the prison itself becomes the community, and the worker is dependent upon services that are available within the institution. Service planning in any resource-poor environment requires considerable ingenuity on the part of the worker to find, adapt, or create the formal and informal services that parents might need.

When services are limited or nonexistent, the worker might want to advocate for the creation of new programs and services that address mothers' needs (see previous chapter). The worker may also look for informal services. Who from the community can or will come into the prison to help?

Services for the child must also be included in case planning. It is important to remember that these children have not only experienced a traumatic separation from a parent but also may have had to cope with a chaotic family life, a new temporary family, and the pain and stigma of a parent's crime and incarceration. As a result, these children may have multiple treatment needs. A previous chapter has already discussed some of the programs available to them in the community. In addition, children are often included in institutionally based programs. Thus, the worker should also be aware of any available programs and refer the child as appropriate.

Service Accessibility

Once the worker has found what services are available, he or she also needs to know how to make them accessible to the parent. What are prison or other service providers' rules around use of services? How are referrals made and who may refer? What is the parent's daily schedule, and does that inhibit service usage? How does the worker coordinate with the service provider to establish treatment goals for the parent? What restrictions does the prison have on bringing in "informal" services?

While access barriers will certainly occur, in some ways access may be enhanced within the prison. The parent is closer to services, may find it easier to keep appointments, and is not as apt to be sidetracked by competing activities or stresses. The worker will thus want to capitalize on these advantages while addressing obstacles. In terms of including children, many of the institutionally based programs focused on children also provide or facilitate transportation to the facility.

Example Programs

Treatment of the incarcerated parent has a dual focus—how to live within the law and provide a safe and stable home for the child. While it is important for the worker to understand this dual focus, in reality there is considerable overlap. Certainly, the life problems associated with commission of a crime and with incarceration overlap with those associated with child maltreatment. These often include poverty, lack of education, alcohol and drug abuse, family violence, and lack of employment. Thus, treatment for one problem is partially treatment for the other, and positive outcomes in one realm coincide with positive outcomes in the other.

One specific way the two focuses overlap is around parenting. Parenting is such an important life role for many inmates that becoming more effective as a parent can be a strong motivator for improvement in other areas. The improving relationships with her children can support a parent's desire to create a safe and stable home and thus to work on problems such as substance abuse and criminal activity. Thus, many of the institutional programs for women are multifaceted, including such services as support for visitation, parenting training, literacy, job skills, and life skills. In addition, because the best way to teach parenting is through observing actual parent-child interactions, many programs bring mothers and their children together and may also have special child-specific elements.

Here are a few examples of programs for mothers and their children:

- **Bedford Hills and Taconic Nursery Programs.** Designed for mothers who deliver during their periods of incarceration, these programs in New York enable mother and infant to live together for periods up to one year or 18 months. Programming includes prenatal care and postpartum classes on such topics as nutrition, immunization, infant development, and parenting; and substance abuse treatment [Gabel & Girard 1995].

- **Children's Visitation Program (CVP).** This Michigan program provides a child-centered environment for visitation, weekly support groups, and parenting classes [Bloom & Steinhart 1993].

- **Centerforce Parent Project.** This program provides case management services, group and individual counseling, and parenting classes to incarcerated women in county jail settings and provides community and home-based services to their children and caregivers during the mother's detention. Follow-up services to the family are also provided after the mother's release [Centerforce 1999].

- **Prison MATCH (Mothers, Fathers, and Their Children).** This program enables children to visit their incarcerated parents for extended (at least 4-hour) periods at a Children's Center, where they engage together in recreational activities. Birthdays and holidays are celebrated, and MATCH staff take Polaroid pictures of parent and child, who are allowed to keep the pictures. MATCH also facilitates children's transportation to the program, assists with the activities, and offers parenting instruction [Brooks & Bahna 1994].

- **The Turning Point Alcohol and Drug Program.** Open to substance abusing women in a minimum security institution, the program provides basic life skills training, substance abuse education, relationship development, and anger management training. Addiction services may also be offered in this Portland, Oregon, program [Morash, et al. 1998].

- **Motherread.** This program for incarcerated mothers in the North Carolina Prison system provides literacy classes in which mothers read and write stories about themselves and their children. During visits, children and other family members may also participate [Brooks & Bahna 1994].

- **Girl Scouts Beyond Bars (GSBB).** A model program implemented in several states, GSBB was created to involve mothers in their daughters' lives during the mothers' period of incarceration. The special Girl Scout troops hold every other meeting in the correctional facility, where girls and their mothers work together on recreational and educational projects, which might include such things as aerobics, arts and crafts, violence prevention, substance abuse, relationships, and teen pregnancy prevention [Block & Potthast 1998].

Special Needs of Caregivers

When a parent is incarcerated, it is the temporary caregiver of her children who provides the milieu in which the child will proceed with developmental tasks while dealing with this trauma. Yet the caregivers themselves may have significant needs that, if unmet, will undermine their ability to care for the child. Thus, it is important that the worker understands their needs and helps them find resources.

Developing Better Supports for Kinship Families

More than 50% of incarcerated mothers and more than 10% of incarcerated fathers report having at least one child living with a grandparent. In addition, from 24% to 44% (depending upon state or federal facility) of incarcerated mothers, and from 3% to 5% of incarcerated fathers report having at least one child living with other relatives (excluding the child's mother or father) or friends [Hostetter & Jinnah 1993]. Often, these are informal arrangements and child welfare agencies are not involved. The child welfare system refers to these arrangements as informal kinship care. At other times, though, child welfare agencies are responsible for placing a child with relatives and for assessing, monitoring, and supervising kinship homes. These arrangements are referred to as formal kinship care. In both formal and informal kinship care, families are referred to as kinship families. Child welfare agencies have a responsibility to provide supports and services for formal kinship families and may also offer supports and services to the informal kinship families who seek them out.

While kinship care has some similarities to nonrelative foster care, there are also many differences. These differences are most likely to be due to the complex web of relationships that exists within families. For better or worse, family members have a history with one another, and experiences from the past are ever present, giving added meaning to relationships. In addition, because one sees family as "part of me," there is greater ego involvement and investment in what family members do. One may feel proud or embarrassed by the actions and lives of other family members. Even more important, one may be frightened that oneself or other family members may repeat the problems of the incarcerated family member.

In addition, the web of kinship moves us to love family members and to care about their futures. But the love and care can, when demands exceed coping ability, be undermined by resentment.

These factors about kinship can work for or against the child in care. On the positive side, they explain much of why kinship care is such a popular placement option today. We believe that this history, connection, involvement, and caring will, all else being equal, result in a better living situation for a child than life with strangers. On the other hand, some people fear that the family problems that resulted in a parent's incarceration and a child's placement in out-of-home care could perhaps be a negative influence on the child in kinship care. What is certain is that the factors intensify the emotions around the placement and bring a new element into the child welfare worker's relationship with child, parent, and substitute caregiver.

Sometimes a child may already have spent much time in the kin's home, even before the incarceration, and kin may already do most of the parenting.

When this is the case, the trauma of the parent's absence may be less severe, but the added element of the incarceration still brings issues to be addressed.

Kinship Foster Family Needs. Despite the generosity and dependability of many of these families, they may be unprepared to deal with the child's placement with them, which will certainly change family life and resurrect or fuel family issues. A caregiver may have to quit a job or change a work schedule to care for the child, straining an already marginal family budget. Family relationships between spouses, among children, and between adults and children will shift. New caregiving tasks will be required. The family may have to learn to interact with two new systems—child welfare and corrections. In addition, the child will bring them into contact with the schools and a range of treatment providers. Thus, families may reach financial, emotional, and responsibility overload.

Thus, the worker should be prepared to help the family cope with the initial crisis of the parent's incarceration and the child's placement and the ongoing presence of the child in their home. The worker can help them understand the shifting relationships in the family. For example, if another child in the home begins to show behavior changes, the caregivers need help in understanding that this may be a result of the new family configuration. If the overload affects spousal or partner relationships, the worker can help the caregivers understand the difficulties as situational rather than as anyone's failure and can help them find appropriate counseling.

Kinship caregivers may have feelings toward the incarcerated parent that interfere with effective caregiving [Hairston 1999]. They may be embarrassed by the parent's behavior or angry with the parent for disappointing the family as well as the child. They may feel resentful that the parent's failure has necessitated their having to cope with the challenges of caregiving. In the face of anger and frustration, it may be difficult to put the child's needs first; they may want to keep the child from the parent to punish the parent or to protect the child and themselves from further disappointment [Hairston 1999]. Alternatively, some caregivers may actively encourage contact between parents and children because they continue to have hope that the parent will one day be able to resume care of the child [Hairston 1999]. Whatever the dynamic, the worker can help caregivers to understand the difference between their own issues and the child's needs for emotional support, honesty, and some sort of contact with the parent. This understanding can help caregivers put the child's needs first, despite their own anger or other complex feelings directed toward the parent.

The financial burden of providing care for the child of an incarcerated parent may be more than anticipated. Often financially strapped even without the addition of the child, the kinship family may find it difficult to provide for the child's basic needs, much less such "extras" as transportation to the correctional facility for visits or treatment for the child. Thus, the worker needs to help the family decide what type of kinship care they would like to offer, since different arrangements carry different financial opportunities and access financial services for which they or the child might be eligible.

The previous chapter on community services gives examples of programs available to help caregivers cope more effectively with the demands of providing care to the child of an incarcerated parent.

Child's Treatment Needs. The kinship foster family must understand that in addition to the usual needs for food, shelter, clothing, and parenting, the child may have treatment needs. These can affect behavioral expectations, discipline, and the kin's role in helping the child deal with separation, shame, and embarrassment associated with incarceration. The family must also be willing to cooperate with the service providers and possibly attend treatment with the child if the child is having trouble adjusting to the new home.

Earlier in this chapter we looked at special institutionally based programs for incarcerated mothers and their children, and the caregiver needs to support the child's attendance at such programs. In addition, other programs specifically for the child, such as school-based support groups, may be available in the community. Mental health services are available in all states and counties, but counselors may or may not have special expertise in working with such children. If the child welfare worker refers a child for mental health services, he or she might want to act as a liaison between the treatment provider and the kinship family, working with the provider on the child's needs and with the family on how to implement treatment suggestions.

Developing Better Supports for Nonrelative Foster Families

Approximately 10% of the children of incarcerated mothers and 2% of the children of incarcerated fathers are living in nonrelative foster homes. [Beck et al. 1992]. These are formal arrangements. The families are foster families who have been licensed by the state to accept foster children, and they may include other foster children in addition to the one being placed. While the issues associated with kinship care are not present in these placements, the strangeness and unfamiliarity of the home and family do present adjustment problems for the child (these are well covered in other literature and won't be repeated here).

Though we have insufficient data on the special needs associated with placement in a nonrelative foster home due to incarceration of a parent, anecdotal reports suggest that many of the needs are the same as those in kinship placements. Foster parents may still be angry with the parent for the impact that her crime and incarceration has on her child. In addition, they may hold stereotypes about crime and criminals that could undermine their work with the children and make it difficult for them to relate to the parent. In addition, it may be logistically difficult for the foster family to facilitate parent-child contacts, with institutions often at a distance from the foster home and collect calls being expensive. When foster parents do take children to prison visits, they may be unprepared for what they will experience and what they will be bringing the child to experience. In addition, they may not understand the dynamics of the visits and the child's reactions nor know how to handle these. Last, the child will probably have special treatment needs of which the foster parents must be aware.

While there are few, if any, specialized support programs for these foster parents, agencies could fill this void by developing and providing special training.

Interventions, Suggestions, and Practice Tips

As a context for effective practice, it is crucial that agency administrators recognize parental incarceration as a special challenge facing workers and the families they serve. At the outset, agency administrators must take responsibility for establishing policies and procedures that support workers who work with these families; making special allowances in terms of caseload, time, and resources; and providing specific training for staff. Criminal justice system staff might be included in that training, both to provide information about the criminal justice system and to learn about the concerns of the child welfare staff [Seymour 1998].

Here is a summary of the practice approaches or strategies that a worker should consider in working with incarcerated parents:

- Prepare yourself to work effectively with the criminal justice system as well as with the parent, her child, and caregivers.
  - Deal with your own feelings around the parent's crime and incarceration. Negative feelings can send messages to the parent and child that will interfere with treatment.
  - Sensitize yourself to prison conditions. You may feel very threatened and uncomfortable when you first visit, but you must address

these feelings before you take a child to visit, since you'll want to adequately prepare him or her.

— Understand and be empathetic to the needs of the prison system. The structure and restrictiveness may look unnecessary to you, but they are functional for the institution. In addition, you may perceive attitudes of prison personnel that upset you. But these are usually ways of coping with stressful jobs and the ever-present security issues within the institution. Find commonality with those within the system and work toward negotiating shared perspectives.

— Establish your own communication channels. Whether or not formal agency-to-agency channels have already been established, you will need your own personal relationships with correctional system staff to guide you through the system, provide access to information, and facilitate your work with the incarcerated parent.

• Support visitation and other forms of contact between parent and child.

— Facilitate visits. Know visiting procedures and restrictions of the institution and prepare the child and caregiver for what it will be like to visit the prison.

— Help the parent and child use visits productively. Talk with the parent before the visit to help her focus on the purpose of the visit and how she and her child can get the most from it. If you are taking the child to the institution, you might need to coach the child before the visit and counsel the child afterward.

— Educate the caregivers regarding the importance and dynamics of visitation. Though they may want to protect the child from the parent and from the prison environment—citing the child's behavior and mood before, during, and after visits as reason for discontinuing visits—caregivers need to understand that the importance to the child of supporting the parent-child relationship overrides those concerns.

— Prepare the caregivers for working with a child effectively before and after a visit. The child already traumatized by the parental crime and incarceration is further traumatized by visitation. While the visit is important for supporting the parent-child relationship, it also will probably be frightening. The child may have ongoing reactions to the visit, not just immediately following the visit. The worker needs to help the caregiver know how to prepare the child for the visit, giving the child some idea of what to expect and assuring the child that it is all right to talk about his or her reactions. Then the caregiver needs to know how to understand the child's post-visit behavior, help the child express the thoughts and emotions behind the behavior, validating the child's emotions as being reality based, and help the child talk about all positive aspects of the visit.

— Offer concrete support around visitation. The distance many families will have to travel to visit the incarcerated parent may be great and the availability or cost of transportation an issue. Provide and/or help them find community assistance with transportation to the prison.

— Facilitate other forms of communication. Know procedures and restrictions around telephoning and exchanging letters, and encourage the family to use these forms of communication within required limitations. In addition, help parents, children, and caregivers discover creative means of keeping their relationships alive, such as making audio tapes, engaging in creative writing, or sharing pictures.

— Understand the agency's responsibility concerning visitation. While you will want to support caregivers in facilitating parent-child contact, ultimately it is the agency's responsibility to insure that parent-child contact occurs. Not addressing the obstacles around visitation may be considered a failure of the agency's "reasonable efforts" requirement.

• Work collaboratively to find services to enable the incarcerated parent to meet permanency planning goals.

— Know what services are available inside the prison and how to access them. Special services could include substance abuse treatment, parenting classes, or educational opportunities (Katz 1998). Know the requirements for participation, and help the parent meet those requirements as appropriate.

— Collaborate with other organizations to provide services not available within the prison. Other community groups may be able to provide such services as transportation to the facility, support for caregivers, or supports for the parent.

— Work with prison social workers to provide coordinated services for children and parents. Work with the correctional staff around holistic planning and service provision so that permanency planning services and rehabilitation services are complementary in preparing the parent for eventual reentry into the community.

- Support the parent and caregiver in working together to meet the needs of the child.
  - Help the family support a positive view of the parent. The family needs to understand that, regardless of what the parent might have done or how they feel about it, the child needs a realistic but positive view of the parent. The worker should be prepared to give them suggestions or help them compose the right words to say to the child. This effort includes helping the child and family members create a cover story that gives honest information to those who are curious about the child's presence in the home while protecting the child's privacy.
  - Help the family put the child's needs first. Family members' negative feelings about the incarcerated parent could result in a range of behaviors toward the child that are not helpful. Behaviors such as withholding parent-child communication, criticizing the parent, and squabbling over the child might "punish" the incarcerated parent, but also punishes the child.
  - Help the family understand the child's immediate needs for support, protection, and information. Caregivers need to know what separation and uncertainty mean to a child emotionally. They also need to understand what the child may experience as a result of his or her own reactions and the reactions of others to the crime and sentence. In addition, they need to be aware of behavioral signs indicating that the child is having problems that need attention. They may also need help in knowing what and how to tell the child about the placement and incarceration.
  - Help caregivers understand the child's possible need for further treatment and help them locate and access such treatment. Help them discover prison or community services geared specifically toward helping children with incarcerated parents.

- Support kinship and nonrelative temporary caregivers.
  - Help the caregivers, particularly kinship caregivers, recognize, understand, and cope with the family crisis. A flood of emotions, tasks, and changes in lifestyle for the whole family are associated with taking on a new member while simultaneously dealing with both the child welfare and criminal justice systems. Family needs at this point may include support, information, treatment, and resources.
  - Help caregivers take care of their own family as they take care of the child. Though the placement is for the child, and his or her needs must come first, family members cannot provide an

adequate home for a child when their unmet needs are great. Thus, they need permission to take care of themselves and to know that self-care does not equate with selfishness. When they are feeling overburdened, they need such assistance as community support groups or respite. They may need family counseling themselves.

— Be prepared to mediate relationships between the family and the incarcerated parent. If negative feelings and negative family dynamics begin to create an environment that is unhealthy for the child or threaten the placement, be prepared to mediate the relationship and help them refocus on the needs of the child.

— Mediate between foster family and incarcerated parent. If communication between foster parents and the mother is blocked, the worker can help each understand and accept the other's role in the child's life and help them work together more effectively for the child.

— Link foster caregivers with community support groups. If no groups are available for foster parents, look for groups for kinship caregivers that will also accept foster parents.

• Work collaboratively on permanency planning from the beginning.

— Involve caregivers in long-term planning for the child. From the beginning of the placement, parent, caregiver, and worker need to work together toward a permanent arrangement for the child. There are many issues to consider, such as the preincarceration relationship between parent and child, the expected length of the incarceration, how long the kin can realistically care for the child, and the foster parent's feelings about and capacity for long-term care of the child should reunification not be a viable option.

— Work closely with institutional staff on prerelease planning. Though there may be uncertainty about when a parent may be released and the conditions of release, working with institutional staff will better help parent, child, and caregiver prepare adequately. [Beckerman 1998].

• Conduct ongoing risk assessment. Whether the child is in a kinship or nonrelative foster home, conduct ongoing risk assessment to ensure the child's safety [Seymour 1998].

Chapter 8

Practice Needs: Permanency Planning Services and Decision-Making

As stated previously, the purpose of out-of-home placement is to provide temporary protection and nurturance for the child while preparing both child and parent for reunification or another permanent arrangement. This purpose is accomplished through a service plan, which states a permanency planning goal and specifies what various parties need to do and must accomplish during a particular period of time to achieve the permanency-planning goal.

The permanency goal of choice is always reunification unless there is a clearly justifiable reason to the contrary. The fact that a parent is incarcerated does not alter the presumption that children belong with their parent(s). Theoretically, this assumption is based on ideas about the importance of bonding and attachment. Children form attachments to their initial caregivers and to other early meaningful figures. Disrupting these attachments has serious consequences that may include, depending upon other factors (e.g., age of the child when the disruption occurs and length of separation) such things as failure to thrive, impaired ability to form later attachments, and depression. Legally, this preference for reunification is stated in federal law (the Adoption Assistance and Child Welfare Act of 1980, P.L. 96-272; the Family Preservation and Support Services Act in 1993, P.L. 103-66) and in most state laws.

Reunification is not always possible. Parents are not always able to provide their children with homes that conform to society's understanding of an adequate home—one characterized by safety, permanence, and stability. Or they may not be able to provide such a home within a timeframe that is suitable to meet a child's developmental needs. The child welfare field is very sensitive to a child's experience of time, which is different from an adult's, and recognizes that children's developmental needs cannot be put on hold while parents rehabilitate. Thus, when either it is initially apparent that a parent cannot provide an adequate home for a child or it is subsequently decided that the parent cannot provide such a home within certain time-frames, the permanency planning goal is no longer reunification but rather another permanent arrangement—adoption, guardianship, or, in some circumstances, permanent foster care.

Thus, one of the most important aspects of child welfare work is decision-making regarding the permanency-planning goal. This has lifelong, often irrevocable consequences for the child, parent, and other caregivers. The worker is called upon to gather and weigh a body of evidence to support a recommendation that may result in a parent and child resuming life together or experiencing various degrees of permanent separation. The worker must make this recommendation within a context that (a) puts the child's safety, permanence, and well-being first; (b) recognizes and respects parental rights; and (c) involves a commitment from the worker and agency to provide reasonable efforts to help a parent achieve the least intrusive goal that is consistent with the child's best interests.

This decision-making is an onerous responsibility under any circumstances. When a parent is incarcerated, however, it becomes more difficult and raises special issues. For instance, constraints around the worker's ability to contact the mother, the artificial environment in which the worker may observe mother and mother-child interactions, difficulties around reasonable efforts, and uncertainties about time of release are obstacles to assessing and planning. This chapter will explore the difficulties and issues associated with assessment of an incarcerated parent and her child for reunification or for other permanency options when reunification has been ruled out. It will begin with a discussion of the Adoption and Safe Families Act of 1997, which sets the context for decision-making. This is followed by discussions of permanency planning for reunification, for termination of parental rights (TPR) and adoption, and for other permanency options and by practice tips.

Adoption and Safe Families Act of 1997

Permanency planning must be viewed within the context of current federal legislation. Generally, the Adoption and Safe Families Act of 1997 (ASFA), P.L.105-89, aims toward moving children more quickly through the child welfare system and making TPR and adoption more easily achieved by shortening timeframes for permanency planning and specifying when states may initiate TPR without having to make reasonable efforts. Various states have enacted additional legislation that further defines decision-making around permanency planning, and case law is enhancing our interpretation of the legislation. The following summarizes these provisions around timeframes and TPR and then looks at implications for permanency planning with incarcerated mothers.

Timeframes

In consideration of the detrimental effects on children of prolonged periods of separation from parents, ASFA specifies shortened timeframes for permanency planning. While previous federal legislation did not require states to initiate TPR proceedings based upon length of stay in care, ASFA stipulates that states must file for TPR on behalf of any child who has been in care for 15 of the most recent 22 months. States must also file for TPR when a parent has abandoned an infant (according to state definition); committed murder or voluntary manslaughter of another child of the parent; or aided and abetted, attempted, conspired or solicited to commit murder or voluntary manslaughter of any child of the parent.

However, the legislation also specifies exceptions to the mandatory filing. Exceptions can be made if:

1. at the state's option, a relative is caring for the child;

2. the state agency documents in the case plan, available for court review, a compelling reason why filing is not in the best interest of the child; or

3. the state agency has not provided to the child's family, consistent with the time period in the case plan, the services deemed necessary to return the child to a safe home.

The new law also establishes that a permanency hearing for children in care must be held within 12 months of a child's entry into care. At that hearing, the determination will be made as to whether and when a child will be returned home, placed for adoption, or referred for legal guardianship or another permanent living arrangement.

Bypassing Reasonable Efforts toward Reunification

Normally, the permanency planning goal of choice is reunification until reasonable efforts to reunify the family have been made and reunification has been ruled out. ASFA requires, as did the earlier P.L. 96-272, that states make "reasonable efforts" (defined variously or not defined by the states) to preserve and reunify families. However, the newer legislation emphasizes that safety, permanency, and well-being are the primary concerns and defines some cases in which reasonable efforts are not required. In other words, the federal law names situations in which reunification does not have to be the goal of choice, and the state may bypass reunification and proceed to another permanency plan. Thus, the reasonable efforts requirement does not apply if a court has found any of the following:

- the parent had subjected the child to "aggravated circumstances" as defined in state law (including but not limited to abandonment, torture, chronic abuse, and sexual abuse);

- the parent has committed murder or voluntary manslaughter or aided or abetted, attempted, conspired, or solicited to commit such a murder or manslaughter of another child of the parent;

- the parent has committed a felony assault that results in serious bodily injury to the child or another one of his or her children; or

- the parental rights of the parent to a sibling have been involuntarily terminated.

Issues and Implications

While ASFA does not dramatically change permanency planning, it does radically alter planning timeframes in ways that will have implications for permanency planning with incarcerated parents. Some of the considerations, issues raised, and possible implications are as follows:

- The above exceptions do not preclude reasonable efforts toward reunification, but rather allow that they may be bypassed. In fact, it is unclear how much these provisions change current practice. Most states already allow agencies to bypass reasonable efforts if they deem that reunification is detrimental to the children. In most cases, agencies have already been foregoing reunification in the third scenario—felony assault resulting in serious bodily injury.

- When working with incarcerated parents, the important thing to remember in making a decision to bypass reasonable efforts toward reunification is that the same standard that applies to any parent would apply to an incarcerated parent, and the fact of the incarceration should not prejudice the worker toward immediately proceeding to other permanency options.

- Realities of the criminal justice system present challenges for planning with an incarcerated parent within ASFA timeframes, since both sentences and time served are apt to be longer than the timeframes allowed by ASFA [Genty 1998]. In addition, a mother may have had children in care and been working on a reunification plan prior to her incarceration, and those months in care also would count toward the 15-month time limit. Thus, many incarcerated parents are faced with an involuntary 15-month separation from their child, regardless of their desire or ability to parent, and with the probability that the child will experience the 15 months in care.

- Because many children of incarcerated mothers are cared for by relatives, there is the option of not filing for TPR despite time in care. (Note that TPR is not precluded, but filing a petition is not mandatory in this situation.) The worker needs to understand this important consideration clearly and ensure that families understand so as to make an informed permanency planning decision.

- The central difficulty around permanency planning with incarcerated parents is the juxtaposition of (a) the rights of the parent, involuntarily separated from the child for a period that may exceed the statutorily determined time limit of 15 months, and (b) the best interests of the child, for whom the length of separation is only one factor.

  — Difficulties imposed around timeframes and obstacles to service delivery render the incarcerated parent particularly vulnerable to inappropriate TPR. Thus, it is essential to understand and protect parental rights. Failure to do so would not only be unfair to the parent but also could harm the child through unnecessary permanent separation from the parent and/or result in the court's ruling against TPR when TPR might have been the best outcome for the child.

  — On the other hand, the well-being of the child is paramount. How long is too long for a child to wait, regardless of the parent's desire to provide a permanent home? Even if the temporary caregiver is a relative, at some point the arrangement needs more permanence. Going beyond the 15-month timeframe on the basis of best interests of the child requires careful consideration and documentation. Thus, we need to consider carefully what permanency should look like for children with incarcerated parents, given what we know about child development, parent-child attachment, a child's sense of time, and a child's need for safety, security, and consistent, sustaining relationships; and we need to consider how the need for permanency can be reconciled with a parent's lengthy prison sentence [Seymour 1998].

One other aspect of ASFA deserves mention. Though the legislation does not specifically address substance abuse in relation to TPR, it does recognize substance abuse as an important issue and states that the Secretary of Health and Human Services will prepare and submit a report, including recommendations for legislation, regarding substance abuse and child welfare. Meanwhile, many states have passed legislation regarding the problem, and these state laws have serious implications for incarcerated mothers, particularly those who have used substances during pregnancy.

Assessing for Reunification

If the permanency planning goal is reunification, the worker, parent, child, and substitute caregiver become involved in creating and implementing a plan that will specify each person's tasks within a set timeframe. The worker's dual role is to make reasonable efforts to assist the parent to achieve the reunification goal while continually assessing the parent's ability to provide a safe and stable home for the child. At a particular time, the worker must either recommend that reunification occur or recommend that the agency proceed with another permanent plan.

Assessing for reunification when a parent is incarcerated poses unique difficulties relating to the legal requirements regarding bypassing reasonable efforts and timeframes, determining the best interest of the child, reasonable efforts toward reunification, in vitro assessment, recidivism issues, and difficulties of reunification.

Screening Against Federal Requirements

The worker should begin the assessment by screening the mother against the provisions of the federal legislation.

The first issue to be taken under consideration would be the mother's crime. Since most women are incarcerated for nonviolent crimes, it is likely that reunification would not be ruled out based upon nature of the crime. Even if the nature of the crime does require consideration of bypassing reasonable efforts, the decision is not automatic, and the worker will still want to ensure that there are no extenuating circumstances that would suggest pursuing reunification.

Next, the worker would want to look at timeframes. Was the child in care before the incarceration? What is the anticipated period of incarceration? If it looks as though the separation will exceed 15 of the past 22 months, do any of the exceptions come into play? Since children are often in temporary care with kin, this would provide the opportunity for proceeding with a plan for reunification. In addition, even if the child is in temporary care with a nonrelative, the plan may still be for reunification if it is judged to be in the best interests of the child. However, when an extended period of incarceration is anticipated, the worker needs to think carefully about how to assess the best interests of the child.

Judging the Best Interest of the Child

According to the second exception, even where the worker anticipates that a child will be in care for 15 or more months of the last 22, petitioning for TPR can be avoided if the child welfare agency documents a compelling reason why filing for TPR is not in the best interest of the child. How would a worker identify a compelling reason that TPR was not in the best interests of the child? How would the worker determine that, despite an extended period of separation, the child's best interests are served if the mother retains custody and reunification is considered?

The worker can begin to evaluate best interests in early contacts with the parent, and ongoing work with the parent provides additional and perhaps more accurate assessment information. While there is no simple and definitive answer to the questions raised above, here are some factors to be considered.

- **Quality of parent-child relationship before incarceration.** A strong and positive preincarceration parent-child relationship would indicate that continuing that relationship might be in the child's best interests. On the other hand, sometimes the lives of parents and their children have been so chaotic due to crime and drugs, or the parent may have been so deprived of nurturance herself, that no viable parent-child relationship ever existed. In other instances, a relationship may have once existed but deteriorated over the years as the parent became increasingly involved in illegal activities and substance use. If there was never a viable relationship, while one may be empathetic concerning the mother's ongoing deprivation, the primary concern is the child, who needs a caregiver who has the capacity to provide ongoing nurturance. If there was once a relationship, the worker will want to assess the reasons for the deterioration and whether or not there is any reason to believe that the relationship can be reestablished through treatment during and after the incarceration [Genty 1998]. Information about the quality of the preincarceration relationship must be carefully documented.

- **Ability to maintain an emotional relationship despite the physical separation.** A strong, positive parent-child relationship may exist despite a parent's criminal activity and incarceration. In this case, the parent's ability to maintain and/or enhance that relationship during incarceration will add to the evidence that eventual reunification may be in the child's best interests. Thus, early in the worker's contact with the parent, he or she should be looking for signs that the parent can and will use this period of incarceration productively. Clearly, supporting the parent-child relationship takes some effort on the part of the worker and all parties involved. It is important that the worker not interpret difficulties related to visitation and other forms of contact as the mother's lack of desire or ability for a positive relationship. As described in the previous chapter, the worker needs to understand the barriers—physical and psychological—and help all parties overcome and work through them [Beckerman 1998].

- **Potential for creating and maintaining a safe and stable home following incarceration.** Though a parent may love her child and may desire an ongoing relationship, a projection that the parent, upon release, would not be able to maintain a safe and stable home for a child would indicate that reunification would not be in the child's best interests. Provision of a safe and stable home would include ensuring that a child had such things as adequate housing, food, medical care, and protection from danger (including exposure to crime). Assessment of these factors can be difficult within the institutional setting, but the worker would want to consider the parent's past behavior, any tangible signs of change, the parent's ability to plan realistically, and the parent's attempts to address problems such as substance abuse.

- **Projected length of incarceration.** When a child has been in care for 12 months and the worker must prepare for a hearing that will determine whether or not the plan continues to be reunification, the parent's projected time for release should be considered. If release is imminent, timing is less of an issue. If an extended period of incarceration is projected, time does become an issue because, despite the mother's best intent, she will not be available for physical care of the child, and one should question how well a parent can psychologically nurture a child under these conditions. Unfortunately, it may be difficult for the worker to project the actual period of incarceration or to obtain the most basic information about the actual sentence, eligibility for parole, or expected release date [Women's Prison Association 1996].

- **Feelings of the child.** In considering the best interest of the child, the worker should consult the child, always communicating at an age-appropriate level [Beckerman 1998]. The child will have a range of confusing thoughts and feelings about the parent and her incarceration, including feelings of responsibility for the incarceration, unrealistic fantasies of family life upon release [Stanton 1980], and/or feelings of shame, embarrassment, and anger [Hannon et al. 1984]. Only by helping the child sort out these feelings can the worker come to an honest understanding of the child's view. For instance, a child's crying and clinging after a visit or an assertion that he or she never wants to see the parent again is not definitive in terms of the child's view.

If the worker determines that, under the federal law, (1) bypassing reasonable efforts is not indicated and (2) either the separation is not projected to be 15 or more consecutive months or there is a good reason (relative placement or best interest of child) to proceed with a plan of reunification, then the worker and parent must prepare a treatment plan and begin to make reasonable efforts toward that goal.

Reasonable Efforts

ASFA requires that states make reasonable efforts toward reunification except under the circumstances previously described. This means that the state must provide services that are needed for a child to return home safely. Indeed, according to the third exception to a mandatory TPR petition, the state child welfare agency's failure to provide such services negates the requirement for a TPR petition after a child has been in care for 15 of the last 22 months. Thus, as the worker is looking toward the mandated 12-month hearing, he or she must consider what services have been provided by the agency.

While it would be unusual for the agency to admit to nonprovision of services, the child welfare agency could be very vulnerable if the parent legally challenged a decision for TPR when services were inadequate. In fact, TPR petitions have been denied and TPR decisions have been overturned on appeal on the basis of failure to provide services, and courts have held agencies accountable for such things as maintaining visitation and providing treatment services [see, for example, In re Sabrina N. 1998]. However, the definition of reasonable efforts is illusive and varies from state to state. California law provides that services to incarcerated parents may include paying collect calls between parent and child, transportation, visitation, and services to extended family. New York law provides that services may include making arrangements for visits, transportation to visits, and social and rehabilitative services [Genty 1998].

Defining reasonable efforts has always been problematic, and the federal legislation has left it to the states to interpret the term. Many low-resource areas of the country challenge workers' efforts to meet the reasonable efforts requirements in reality, if not under the law. In other words, because of the lack of resources, reasonable efforts may be defined at a level that is inconsistent with the actual needs of families. Defining and meeting reasonable efforts requirements is even more difficult in the case of incarcerated parents. (The previous chapter discussed the difficulty of obtaining services within the prison.) Still, the fact of the parent's incarceration does not excuse the agency from the reasonable efforts requirement. The worker should be sure that he or she has at a minimum made the required periodic contacts with the parent; facilitated visitation, including the transportation; ensured that required services are actually available and accessible to the parent; and ensured that the parent is notified of hearings and is enabled to participate through her actual presence, deposition, or affidavit.

In Vitro Assessment

Another problem in permanency planning with incarcerated parents is that the worker must often make an assessment of a parent's ability to provide a safe and stable home while she is in an artificial setting in which it is difficult to demonstrate parenting and other life skills. Unless the time served is short and the parent will have returned home and had the opportunity to demonstrate stability, the worker must look for signs of good parenting that can be reasonably demonstrated during incarceration. What might the worker look at as evidence that the parent is working successfully toward reunification?

- **Consistent interest in visitation.** The mother's consistent desire to visit her child indicates her desire and expectation for a continuing relationship. In assessing this factor, though, it is important for the worker to ensure that visits are actually available and that he/she has helped child, caregiver, and parent overcome the barriers to visitation.

- **Quality of visits.** The worker should assess how the parent interacts with the child during visits. Are actual changes in parenting behavior evident? The worker's ability to assess the quality of interactions, however, will depend upon conditions at the prison—whether or not contact is allowed, whether there is a quiet and calm place to interact, and whether special programs are available that allow for extended visits or activities. In addition, the extent to which the worker has prepared all parties for the visits will also affect the quality of interactions.

- **Other efforts at communication.** Given the limitations on visiting, what other efforts does the parent make to communicate with the child? Does she try to call or write? Does she take advantage of other creative opportunities that might arise, such as exchanging audio tapes or photographs?

- **Involvement in the child's life.** Does the parent attempt to participate in decision-making regarding the child to the extent allowed through the care arrangement? Does she ask about the child's school, daily activities, behaviors, and progress?

- **Compliance with her treatment program.** Does the mother regularly participate in any recommended treatment, indicating her motivation to parent and ability to maintain some kind of regularity in life? Does she problem solve with the worker around any barriers to her participation in treatment?

- **Involvement in hearings.** Does the parent participate in hearings regarding her future with her child? It is up to the worker to ensure that the mother is notified of hearings and of her rights. However, even if the mother is notified, she may be unable to attend. In such as situation, she needs to be informed of and assisted in exercising her right to participate through deposition or affidavit.

- **Planning for the future.** How realistically is the mother able to think about and plan for her postincarceration life? Does she converse clearly about what will be required of her in terms of preparing a home for the child, and does she suggest convincing strategies for creating a viable home? What are her plans regarding income and a place to live?

- **Facing recidivism.** Does she understand the danger of recidivism, and does she speak convincingly concerning how she expects to avoid recidivism? Does she realistically assess the roles of family support, prosocial friends, and substance use in supporting or endangering her postincarceration adjustment? If she has a history of recidivism, does she have a realistic plan for how this time will be different?

- **Facing past child maltreatment.** If she has a history of child maltreatment, do her behaviors during visits, compliance with treatment, and conversations around parenting indicate that she will be able to parent without maltreatment?

While it is undeniably difficult to assess a parent's skills and strengths during incarceration, especially when there is a history of child maltreatment or serious preincarceration issues, close attention to the above issues will help the worker and mother assess the feasibility of reunification. In addition, planning for a time period in which the parent may establish herself in the community before resuming full care of her child allows an additional margin of safety.

Difficulties of Reunification

We have said that prison is an artificial environment for the parent's demonstration of life skills and ability to provide a safe and stable home, and that this complicates decision-making around permanency planning. But the artificiality of the environment also affects permanency planning in that it shelters the parent. While the prison environment is not easy and has its own stresses, it also provides structure and routine, a place to live, and food while offering the parent some protection from the temptations of criminal activities and substance use.

The worker needs to assess how the parent will function outside the prison, amid the demands and threats of everyday life. Reintegration into the community is always difficult, and without adequate supports, many ex-offenders fail. If treatment during incarceration has been inadequate, parents may return to the community with all the problems they had before plus additional problems resulting from their incarceration—stigma, loss of self-esteem, the effect of exposure to other criminals, and the effect of having been deprived of normal adult responsibilities. In addition, with welfare reform, many will be ineligible for public assistance (e.g., drug felons or those who have already been terminated from TANF). They may have difficulty finding housing and employment, completing a service plan, staying clean, and reunifying with their children all at the same time. (These difficulties will be discussed further in the next chapter.)

Concurrently Planning for Reunification and Adoption

Often at the time a service plan is being drafted, it is impossible to know whether the permanency goal should be reunification or some other arrangement. In addition, unless the conditions for bypassing reunification are met, the parent has the right and opportunity to rehabilitate before the agency proceeds to another option. In the past, this "tiering" effect in permanency planning tended to necessitate a considerable time lag between the time that a permanency goal was changed from reunification to another option. To speed up permanency planning, new legislation and practice favor concurrent planning. While the worker is assisting the parent with meeting a goal of reunification and assessing progress toward that goal, he or she may at the same time be exploring other options and even preparing to file for TPR, particularly if the worker has doubts about the parent's ability to successfully work toward reunification.

In concurrent planning, the worker and mother work toward reunification at the same time they begin the work toward TPR and adoption or legal guardianship. The advantage is that, if the plan should change, it can be accomplished more quickly than if no work on TPR or guardianship had been started. In concurrent planning, though, it is particularly important for the worker to fully disclose to the mother the dual plan, helping her understand the commitment to reunification along with the need for proceeding toward another option should this be necessary to ensure child safety, permanency, and well-being. It may be very difficult for the mother to have to talk about TPR when she is working toward reunification, but the worker must engage her in long-term planning for her child and help her handle the grief that she will no doubt experience. The worker may try to use the concurrent planning process as a motivator, making very real to the parent the necessity for engaging in treatment.

Assessing for Adoption and Other Options

If the decision is made initially or subsequently that reunification is not the plan of choice, the worker and parent must plan for another means of providing long-term care for the child. The most drastic of these, because it is intended as a permanent change of caregiver, is adoption, though other less drastic means—guardianship or, in some cases, permanent foster care—are also options.

Assessing for Adoption

In choosing a permanency plan of adoption and preparing to file for TPR, a worker is asserting that in his or her best judgment, a parent will not be able to provide for the safety, permanency, and well-being of a child within a timeframe consistent with the child's developmental needs, and the best interests of the child are served by a permanent severance of parent-child legal ties. While TPR in some cases may seem unfair to the parent, who may be involuntarily separated from her child for a considerable period of time despite her attachment to her child [Genty 1998], the best interest of the child takes precedence.

Making the decision to file for TPR is enormously important and, although ASFA does make it easier to file for TPR, the legislation also serves to safeguard some parental rights. In addition, court decisions have clarified the importance of procedural safeguards and that a parent's unfitness must be proved by clear and convincing evidence.

While many states are more clearly defining the circumstances in which TPR is appropriate if a parent is incarcerated, most still hold to the notion that incarceration in itself is not to be deemed abandonment and may not be the sole reason for TPR [NCCAN 1997]. On the other hand, factors associated with incarceration may point toward the need for TPR. Generally, the factors that state laws and courts have considered in these cases are as follows:

- **Duration of the separation.** Some states use vague wording to describe a too-long period of separation (e.g., "substantial portion" of childhood) while others give specific timeframes, anywhere from one to ten years.

- **Nature of the crime.** Many state statutes provide that incarceration may be a ground for TPR where the parent has been convicted of a crime—such as murder, battery, sexual abuse—against a child's sibling or other child living in the parent's home. ASFA supports this notion. Some states do not define the kind of crime necessary to support a TPR petition, while other states provide that certain crimes—such as murder or rape—may be grounds for TPR regardless of whether or not the victim was a child.

- **Preincarceration attachment.** Courts are more apt to support TPR if the mother's preincarceration life was chaotic and the parent-child attachment was weak or nonexistent than if a mother and child once had a viable home and relationship together.

- **Age of the child.** Age of the child is considered in terms of the length of absence and the parent-child attachment. For instance, an older child who already has had years of a positive relationship with a parent may be able to endure a prolonged period of separation. In addition, such a child may reach his or her majority in a few years, making brief the period for which permanency planning is relevant. On the other hand, a younger child has had less time to attach and will have more years ahead, during which he or she needs a permanent home.

- **Availability of less intrusive options.** Considering the extreme intrusiveness into family life that TPR represents, courts want to ensure that the goals of child safety, permanency, and well-being cannot be met by a less intrusive option.

- **Procedural requirements.** Even if TPR seems to be the best option, parents' rights are protected by procedural requirements. If these are not followed, the court may not grant TPR.

  While ASFA lays out situations in which the child welfare agency must petition for TPR, in order for the TPR to be granted, the state still must show that the parent is unfit [*Santosky v. Kramer* 1982; *Stanley v. Illinois* 1971]. The U.S. Supreme Court ruled that TPR hearings must be held under a high evidentiary standard: parental unfitness must be proven by "clear and convincing evidence," not just "a preponderance of the evidence" [*Santosky v. Kramer* 1982]. Some of the measures courts might use are the following (note that they closely parallel the factors the worker considers in determining best interests of the child):

- **Ability to meet children's emotional needs.** Because children have many emotional needs, fitness to parent includes the ability to provide love and affection, nurturance, emotional support, roots, and identity. If a relationship was absent and emotional needs were not met before the parent's incarceration, the fact of incarceration may be irrelevant. For example, if the child experienced chronic absence of a parent due to substance abuse or if a parent never attached to a child, there may never have been a viable relationship. But if there was a preincarceration relationship, the separation necessitated by incarceration may be an interlude that holds potential for nurturing and supporting parent-child ties [Genty 1998].

- **Ability to perform the tasks of parenting.** A child's need for permanence and stability includes being able to count on the parent to be a regular and steady caregiver. There should be preincarceration evidence that she provided instruction and guidance to the child and attempted to meet the child's needs for safety and protection. During incarceration, there should be evidence that she was reliable in terms of her efforts to maintain contact with the child, ability to communicate with the child, and ability to follow routines. The parent should also evidence some awareness of the child's emotional and developmental needs.

- **Ability to provide the child's physical needs.** As stated earlier, poverty cannot be construed as child maltreatment or inability to parent, yet if a parent does not take advantage of available resources or cannot use available resources appropriately to create a safe and stable home for the child, parental fitness comes into question. Both preincarceration lifestyle and realistic plans for postincarceration life might be considered as evidence of ability to provide for a child's physical needs.

- **Risks posed by criminal behavior.** Sometimes the parent's criminal behavior itself puts a child at such risk that fitness to parent comes into question. Certainly criminal behaviors against one's own children—killing or maiming a child—speak to parental unfitness. But other behaviors, such as a long history of involvement in crime that daily puts the child in the midst of an environment characterized by criminality, habitual violence, or using the child to conduct criminal acts (e.g., having the child transport drugs) would also suggest a disregard for the child's well-being and thus, parental unfitness. Again, the court would look at preincarceration lifestyle and at any evidence of rehabilitation during incarceration.

• **Effects on child's well-being.** The worker must consider whether a relationship with the parent will undermine a child's safety, permanence, and well-being. Sometimes a parent may desire a continued relationship with a child, but the parent's and child's history together has been so devastating to the child that to continue it would have a deleterious effect on a child's psychological and emotional well-being [Matter of Adoption of Children by L.A.S. 1993, cited in Genty 1998].

The worker must be skilled at not only assessing but also carefully documenting these factors in order to assist the court with making a decision around parental fitness. In addition, the worker will document the results of his or her reasonable efforts (unless there is justification for bypassing them). Thus, the worker needs to document that he or she made the required visits, answered the mother's calls and letters, responded to barriers to visitation and service provision, and provided information about and opportunity to participate in court hearings, and how the parent used these opportunities. Documentation of a parent's use of opportunities for visits, services, or participation in court hearings would then support decision-making around parental fitness or unfitness.

Special Issues

TPR and adoption are drastic but sometimes necessary measures in terms of intrusion into family life, and this is particularly difficult when the parent-child separation is involuntary due to incarceration. Thus, it is important for the worker to help the mother gain some sense of control over her and her child's fate. One way this is done is through maximum involvement of the mother in decision-making from the beginning so that she has the opportunity to see that the TPR decision is a way of giving her best to the child. If, on the other hand, she disagrees with the decision, she will at least have participated in the assessment and will understand how the decision was made. Another way of giving her control is through voluntary relinquishment rather than involuntary termination of parental rights. In this situation, the mother may be able to negotiate an open adoption arrangement where she may continue to have some contact with her child via an agreed-upon schedule of visits or exchange of pictures or letters.

The following special issues complicate assessing for TPR when a parent is incarcerated:

• When attachment between a child and parent is strong, it may be very difficult for the worker and parent to arrive at a decision to file for TPR. Yet, particularly when a child is very young and a sentence is very long, this may be the best plan. In such a situation, the worker might try to capitalize on the strength of the mother's caring for her child to help her want the best for the child.

- When some of the children have special needs, finding adoptive homes may be difficult. While this poses a challenge for the agency, it is not a reason to avoid TPR if it is otherwise indicated.

- When the length of incarceration is the factor preventing reunification but the parent-child relationship is good, the agency might consider open adoption. The mother's inability to physically care for her child does not mean that she has nothing to give emotionally. If the mother has been important in the child's life, it may be to the child's advantage to continue the relationship, though the child has another permanent caregiver.

- When relatives have provided temporary care for a child during the parent's incarceration and it becomes clear that long-term care is needed, relative adoption should be considered. Because many children are residing with grandparents, some dismiss adoption as viable option, considering the more informal kinship arrangement as permanent. In addition, some kinship families are reluctant to adopt because it requires TPR proceedings against the incarcerated family member. While these are considerations, some relative caregivers may welcome the stability of adoption, which adds permanence to the arrangement and gives more rights to the caregivers.

Assessing for Other Options

When reunification is not possible, the family may also consider another permanency option that is not as drastic as TPR and adoption—legal guardianship. This option provides some security and stability for the child by assigning some rights and responsibilities to the caregiver while still preserving parental rights [Seymour 1998]. Legal guardianship is a judicially established relationship between a caregiver and child, which is intended to be permanent. Certain rights with respect to the child are transferred to the caregiver (e.g., protection, education, care and control, and decision-making), but the mother's parental rights are not terminated. Many states now provide subsidies for legal guardians to care for children in their guardianship.

In assessing for legal guardianship as a permanency option, the following factors need to be considered:

- **Permanence and stability.** What degree of permanence and stability does the guardianship provide as opposed to other options?

- **Parental agreement.** Does the parent support the guardianship arrangement such that she can negotiate division of responsibilities and will not disrupt the arrangement?

- **Relationship of caregivers and parents.** Do the kinship caregivers want to avoid TPR, seeing it as so disruptive to their relationship with the parent as to undermine their ability to care for the child?

- **Intrusion into family life.** Is it important to the family to choose an option that minimizes their involvement with the child welfare system and/or legal procedures?

- **Financial needs and assistance.** What are the financial needs of the family in caring for the child, and what does the state offer under various options (i.e., adoption subsidies, foster care payments, guardianship subsidies, all of which will vary from state to state)?

In permanency planning with incarcerated parents and their children, guardianship is most likely to be considered when children are already living with a relative, though the arrangement is also open to nonrelatives. If a child is living in an informal kinship care arrangement with relatives and it appears that the length of incarceration will be extensive, the kin may want to formalize the arrangement. Guardianship would give the caregivers more rights regarding the child than the informal arrangement would provide and would give the child some sense of permanency. In addition, many kinship caregivers find it impossible to support a child without financial assistance, and guardianship may enable them to receive a subsidy.

Guardianship may also be considered if a child is already in a relative foster home. Since foster care is traditionally considered a temporary arrangement, guardianship again might provide a greater sense of permanency. At the same time, it would involve much less intrusion into family life by the child welfare system (e.g., licensing, required training, agency custody, court hearings) than would formal foster care.

Relatives may prefer guardianship over adoption when they would feel uncomfortable or worried about being seen by the parent as a party to TPR. Particularly when the problem is length of incarceration rather than the mother's unfitness to parent, the relatives may see TPR as an overly harsh action. In addition, TPR would become a part of the family history with which all members would have to cope over many years. Kin may have other personal reasons why they don't want to adopt, yet they may still want to provide a home and care for the child. In addition, if the child is an adolescent, he or she may not want to be adopted and thus may prefer guardianship. However, since guardianship does not terminate parental rights, that arrangement would be more vulnerable to a parent subsequently attempting to reclaim the child.

Sometimes permanent foster care with a specified caregiver may be used, particularly when the child is an older adolescent and is looking forward to being on his or her own and has little interest in establishing formal ties with another caregiver. If a child is doing well in a suitable foster home, continuing this arrangement for a longer period of time may be the option of choice. (However, adoption should not be ruled out for older adolescents, since some do want the security and stability of a new family, even if they will be living with the family for only a short while.) If permanent foster care is the permanency option, the worker will want to ensure that appropriate independent living services are offered so that the teenager will be prepared to live independently.

Practice Tips

Given the importance of and inherent difficulties in permanency planning decision-making, additional difficulties created by parental incarceration, and the new context for permanency planning presented by ASFA, child welfare workers need to consider the following:

- When a parent is incarcerated, reunification is the permanency plan of choice unless and until it has been ruled out according to provisions of state or federal legislation.

- Because difficulties with timeframes and obstacles to service delivery render an incarcerated parent particularly vulnerable to TPR, the worker should pay particular attention to reasonable efforts and due process for parents.

- Though assessing an incarcerated parent's potential for reunification is difficult, useful indicators include:
  — preincarceration history of parenting, including meeting the child's emotional, educational, and physical needs;
  — projected timeframes for the incarceration, though this can be difficult to ascertain;
  — child's view of his or her relationship with the parent and desire for reunification;
  — consistency of the parent's interest in visitation;
  — quality of the parent-child visits;
  — the parent's other efforts at communication with the child;
  — the parent's continued interest and involvement in the child's life;

— the parent's compliance with her treatment program;

— involvement of the parent in hearings;

— the parent's ability and willingness to plan realistically for the future;

— the parent's ability and willingness to face the possibility of recidivism and to develop a realistic plan to avoid it;

— the parent's ability and willingness to face any past maltreatment of her child and to develop a plan to avoid it.

• Engage in concurrent planning when reunification hasn't been ruled out but adoption is more likely.

• Consider the following when assessing for TPR and adoption:

— preincarceration attachment, with absence of attachment indicating the need for TPR;

— duration of the separation, with prolonged separation causing such deprivation to a child as to suggest the need for adoption;

— nature of the parent's crime, since some crimes would suggest such ongoing risk to a child as to indicate a need for adoption;

— age of the child, with younger children particularly being in need of a long-term stability and continuity that adoption can provide; and

— the parent's ability to meet the child's emotional and physical needs.

• Involve the parent, child, and caregivers to the maximum degree possible to arrive at a permanency plan that reflects the realities of these families, particularly when reunification is not an option.

• Consider voluntary relinquishment as an option if the parent is able to engage in this kind of planning and decision-making, since this option would allow her to feel more control over her destiny, which could have positive consequences for her future relationships with the child and the child's caregivers (should they agree to open adoption).

• Investigate flexible options, such as open adoption and legal guardianship, that enable the parent to continue a relationship with the child, even where lengthy incarceration may prevent her from providing day-to-day care for the child.

• Encourage agencies to provide child welfare staff with training in establishing permanency goals when a parent is incarcerated.

Chapter 9

Practice Needs: Reunification, Postplacement, and Aftercare Services

Federal law requires that by at least the twelfth month from a child's entrance into care, a dispositional hearing be held to determine whether a child and parent will be reunited or another permanency option will be implemented. The results of the hearing will shape the future work with the parent, child, and others, such as kin and nonrelative caregivers. Regardless of the plan, there will be tasks to complete with each party in preparing, implementing, and supporting the new arrangement. This chapter looks at general issues related to the parent's release and at the special practice issues and needs related to parental incarceration when families reunify, when children remain with kin, and when they are adopted. Finally, practice tips will be offered.

General Issues Surrounding Release

When reunification is the permanency plan, and frequently when kinship care or adoption is the plan, a mother will return to the community. Anyone leaving prison faces challenges in resuming (or beginning) a normal life, a life in which her material needs are met and she experiences satisfying relationships both within her own family and within the community. Whether or not she is reunited with her children, chances are that she will continue to have some kind of relationship with them and will have some role in their lives. Her ability to function as an independent or appropriately interdependent adult in the community is a prerequisite for a successful relationship with her children, whatever the custody and living arrangements, and for resisting recidivism.

Understanding Reentry

To fully appreciate the challenges of reentry, it is necessary to consider what life was like for the parent before incarceration, what she experienced while incarcerated, and what she might return to when she is released.

In terms of preincarceration, we have already seen that incarceration is rarely an isolated event, unrelated to other social and economic problems. More likely than not, the mother was poor, living in a neighborhood characterized by dilapidation and criminal activity. Her educational level and job skills restricted her ability to support herself. She was apt to have been alcohol and/or drug involved and to have experienced some form of abuse from her family of origin and/or from current relationships. Overall, though home life might have been safe and stable, it was more apt to have been chaotic, dangerous, and unpredictable.

The mother's experiences during incarceration for the most part do not prepare her well for reentry. We have already reviewed some of the emotions she may experience—shame, guilt, and anger. We have seen in our discussion of barriers to visitation how it may be difficult for her to continue positive relationships with family members.

Looking then at postincarceration conditions, what might a woman experience? Unless she has received specific help and support, she will return to the conditions she left—conditions of poverty, drug and alcohol abuse, violence, criminally involved associations, poor education, and poor job skills. In addition, if she had a job prior to incarceration, it is now lost, and she may have lost her home. Further, she may have lost the support of family, may bring with her coping styles that are inappropriate to community life, and she certainly brings the stigma of incarceration. Her only friendships may be with other women she met in prison and her formerly criminally-involved friends, and her only recreation may center around establishments where substance abuse and criminality are ever present. While she knows she may be led into further crime without something positive to substitute for these people and places, she will find resisting them impossibly difficult.

Given the obstacles a woman faces upon release, it is no wonder that recidivism is high. While incarceration may provide for a woman a period of stability in which she can collect herself and consider the direction of her life, overall, incarceration seldom is a positive experience. Certainly it is unlikely that she can use the experience well without help. In addition, even if there are positive aspects of incarceration and a woman has made some gains in prison, the transition to the community may erode those gains if adequate supports aren't available.

Planning for and Supporting Reentry

Child welfare professionals may or may not be involved when a woman leaves prison. In fact, most women, even women with children, leave without any child welfare intervention. In such cases, any discharge and transitional planning that exists is in the hands of the corrections and parole systems, and this is likely to be minimal. Their focus will be on defining and monitoring conditions of parole and attempting to avoid recidivism.

When child welfare is involved, interagency collaboration is required to holistically address the woman's social, economic, and other needs so that she may not only successfully remain in the community but also carry out her responsibilities, whatever they may be, in assuring safety, permanence, and well-being for her child.

Though each woman is unique, there are certain things that must be in place for her to reestablish herself in the community, including the following:

- **Housing.** She must have a place to live, but finding housing may be very difficult. If she is able to reside with relatives, this may be a ready and easy solution. On the other hand, if the relatives aren't really prepared for her, she could have a housing crisis within weeks or months. In addition, if the relatives themselves are involved in substances and crime, she will quickly be led astray. On the other hand, she may have no financial resources to live on her own. She may need transitional housing. But whatever options are available, planning should include consideration of stability, appropriateness, and cost of the arrangement.

- **Income and employment.** She must have some means of support. It is unlikely that relatives will be able to help much. If plans are for reunification, welfare benefits—Temporary Assistance to Needy Families (TANF)—if available to her at all, will only be available after she and her children are reunited, putting her in a catch-22: she needs to demonstrate her stability before she reclaims her children, but she has to have her children with her to achieve economic stability through TANF. Time limits and exclusions (such as for felony drug convictions) may make TANF inaccessible to her. In addition, she may have other problems that make it difficult for her to find employment on her own—problems with her mental health or substance abuse, limited education, in addition to her criminal record.

- **Relationships.** The need for appropriate support and companionship from family and friends is great yet not easily achieved, given the woman's possible preincarceration environment of criminality, abusive relationships, and the stigma and negative attitudes toward her due to her incarceration. Continuing her old patterns of relationships may quickly lead to recidivism, but she probably will not know how to form more helpful relationships nor might they be available to her.

- **Other needed treatment.** If the woman was substance involved before incarceration, even if she has received treatment, she will need to immediately connect with community-based treatment before she falls back into her old behaviors. She may also need mental health services, life-skills training, parenting training, and support and assistance in meeting all conditions of parole.

Again, while these elements are needed for anyone's successful readjustment back into the community, they take on particular importance when children are involved. From the child welfare worker's perspective, permanency planning begins at intake, and this doesn't change when the parent is incarcerated. It does, however, become more complicated because of the difficulty of collaboration and meeting the needs of two systems, the barriers to permanency planning already mentioned, and the severe nature of many of the women's problems.

The following sections look at special issues involved in planning for reunification, for kinship care, and for adoption.

Planning for Reunification

When the decision has been made to reunify, much work must be done to support the success of the arrangement. In this situation, the children have been in family foster care, kinship care, or group care (or different children may have been in different arrangements), and a careful assessment has led to the conclusion that the best plan for the children is to return to their mother.

Discharge planning for reunification and successful accomplishment of reunification is not easy. Cross-systems communication may be poor and the child welfare worker may not know when a mother is to be released, and an unplanned release may lead to a period of homelessness. Community resources may be limited, or the mother may have difficulty accessing the programs she needs, leading not only to failure to rehabilitate but also to violation of parole. Another possible scenario is that the mother may feel under such pressure to reunite with her children to prove her worthiness as a mother that she pushes for precipitous reunification, which leads to failure [WPA 1996].

To avoid these problems and to give the mother and her children the best chance for success, the following should be considered:

- Assess the parent's functioning outside the prison, amid the requirements and threats of everyday life. Reintegration into the community can be difficult, and without adequate supports, many ex-offenders fail. If treatment during incarceration has been inadequate, parents may return to the community with all the problems they had preincarceration plus additional ones resulting from the incarceration. It may be difficult to find housing and employment, complete a service plan, stay clean, and reunify all at the same time.

- Organize discharge planning, to be done jointly between the corrections, pardon and parole, and child welfare systems. The mother will have a hard time meeting the demands of pardon and parole plus requirements imposed by the child welfare system if the conditions are contradictory. Conditions of parole may include such things as mandatory alcohol or drug treatment, restrictions on associations, conditions around moving, restrictions regarding the opposite sex, and correspondence with other inmates. The child welfare worker needs to be aware of these and help the mother avoid violating parole.

- Begin work early on transition to parole and postincarceration services. If the mother is to reenter the community successfully, planning has to begin as soon as possible so that necessary services are in time to ensure a smooth transition. If left too late, such things as waiting lists or logistical difficulties may leave the mother unable to access necessary community services.

- Help the mother think rationally during her incarceration about her past and future. We have said that the prison environment provides structure and routine, shelter, and food while offering the parent some protection from the temptations of criminal activities and substance use. Worker and parent together need to discuss what reentry will be like. They need to consider what life was like before the separation, how the period of incarceration may have changed things, what difficulties the parent will face upon reentry, and what supports can help the parent maintain a safe and stable home.

- Help the mother deal with her fears and fantasies around release. Many women are ambivalent about their return to the community. While prison life is hard, life in the community may appear harder. The despised structure of prison life gives way to the awesome responsibility for important adult decision-making, and chaos and failure are always lurking.

- Help the mother express and examine her fantasies around resumption of her role as mother. For many mothers, the prospects of reuniting with their children provided the primary motivation for surviving prison. Yet, however reunification is accomplished, it will not match the fantasy. A mother may have to wait longer than she wants for the reunification. Her children may have reestablished their lives without her and not want to have their new lives disrupted. They may have grown and changed in ways that she hadn't anticipated, or they might hesitate to recommit to her, fearing that she will leave them again. If siblings experienced different placements, the sibling bonds might have weakened. On the other hand, with the passage of time and harsh prison conditions, the mother herself has changed and may not realize the effect this has on her children's ability to reconnect with her. For instance, she may have developed an aggressive stance that may have been functional in prison but not in community life or in mothering.

- Provide assistance with the readjustment to the entire family. If the mother is returning to a three-generational household in which relatives were caring for her children, she herself may be seen as the intruder, and relatives who struggled to make the adjustment of accepting her children may resent her upsetting that hard-won stability by reinserting herself into their family system. She may be seen as upsetting routines, deestablishing the relatives' authority, and negatively influencing the children. The entire family may need assistance for the reunification to be successful.

- Prepare the children for reunification. The children will have endured the pain of separation and come to terms with that, each in his or her own way. Accepting the mother back into their day-to-day lives is not a simple matter of erasing the pain of separation. Rather, it requires another adjustment plus the willingness to risk retraumatization should the mother leave again. How well they make this transition depends upon such things as their prior relationship with her, how that relationship was maintained or changed during the period of incarceration through visits or other contact, their living arrangement during the incarceration, availability of counseling during the pain of separation, and how much the mother has changed [Henriques 1996]. Involve the children, as much as age-appropriate, in decision-making around reunification and keep them informed of any other factors that will affect them.

- Don't reunite the mother and children immediately. Rarely is a woman's transition from prison to the community so smooth that she can reunite with her children immediately. More likely, she will need time to reestablish herself. Remember, too, that the assessment leading to a permanency plan of reunification was made during her incarceration, and some period of proving herself in the community may be advisable. In this case, it is important to be clear with her about projected timelines and exactly what needs to happen before she gets the children back, so she doesn't become discouraged and lose her motivation to stay drug- and crime-free.

When Kinship Care Is the Permanent Plan

Kinship care is a broad term including a range of informal and formal arrangements in which children are cared for by relatives. Sometimes this is a temporary placement. For instance, children may be placed with relatives for the period of their mother's incarceration with the expectation that they will return to her when she is released. The placement may be informally arranged by the mother, or it may be formally arranged by a child welfare agency. The relatives may be designated as guardians and may receive a fee for taking care of the children, or they may be licensed as a family foster home, specifically to care for their kin.

Whether or not permanency was the original intent, the kinship care arrangement may continue during a mother's prolonged incarceration or beyond the mother's release. In fact, the permanent plan may be to continue the kinship care. In this case, the child welfare agency's involvement will depend upon the arrangement. If the arrangement is a guardianship, while the relatives may receive money to support the care arrangement, they do not typically receive services from the agency. Decisions regarding rearing of the child are negotiated between the relative guardians and the mother. This arrangement has advantages in that it may provide financial assistance to kin who would otherwise be unable to care for the children, it allows families to care for their own without having to accept agency monitoring and services, and it continues to involve the mother with raising her children on a limited basis. On the other hand, it is dependent upon the good will of both mother and kin to work together cooperatively for the good of the children. If the mother is unhappy with the children's care and intervenes beyond the agreed terms or tries to take the children away, the arrangement will fail, or if the kin try to exclude the mother, the arrangement will fail. In addition, if the family needs services they are not seeking, the children could suffer.

Child welfare will be more involved with the family if they have become a licensed foster home. In that case, they get financial support, accept monitoring, and participate in needed services, as would any foster parents. The participation of the mother in child rearing may be less than in a guardianship arrangement. Though foster care is meant to be a temporary arrangement rather than a long-term arrangement, in many instances kinship foster care is being used for long-term placements, and there is still disagreement in the child welfare field as to whether or not this is actually a permanency plan option.

Sometimes what begins as a temporary kinship care arrangement actually becomes an adoption, involving termination of parental rights (TPR). In this case, as in any adoption, all parental rights are forfeited, and the kin become the adoptive parents. The kin may receive an adoption subsidy and are eligible for postadoption services from the agency. The extent of the birth mother's involvement with her children (openness of the adoption) is negotiable.

The similarity in all these arrangements is that the mother gives up to other family members some level (depending upon the arrangement) of rights and responsibilities toward her children. In almost all instances, the mother will know where the children are, will expect some access to them, and will be involved in a complex web of family relations. While each of these situations is different, there are some considerations that relate to all.

- The extent of the mother's physical presence in the home will vary. She may actually live in a three-generational home with her children and their kin caregiver, she may live there sporadically, or she may be in and out for visits. On the other hand, if she continues in long-term incarceration, she may never be physically present in the home. In any case, it is important that her presence and/or involvement be supportive of the children's safety, permanence, and well-being rather than undermining it. Considerable negotiation of new family boundaries, roles, responsibilities, needs, and expectations may be necessary. In addition, children need to understand and be able to explain to others the care arrangement.

- As with other scenarios, the whole family needs help in seeing the mother in a positive light. This is not to deny the reality of crime and or/criminal lifestyle, but to recognize the importance to the children of a positive view of this person who was not able to withstand the disadvantages and pressures of her life but still wanted the best for her children.

- If she has returned to the community, the mother may be present in the home much of the time or be in and out. This may confuse the children about their relationship with her and about their future relationship. Thus, they need to understand that her repeated returns to the home don't mean that they will be returning to live with her.

- The mother may need help with handling her feelings about her inability to reunite and help with her new role if she still has contact with her children. She may be feeling grief over the loss of her children, shame and guilt regarding her failure, and anger toward those who are replacing her. She may need help in handling her feelings as well as in deciding how she will handle her loss with others—her own cover story that does not brand her as a bad mother. The more she has been able to participate in decision-making, the better able she will be to retain her self-esteem and sense of control in relation to care arrangements other than reunification.

- If she has returned to the community, the mother's ability to function in any capacity with her children may depend upon her ability to use substance abuse treatment. The child welfare worker, parole officer, and family all need to support her getting such treatment. They need to understand the role that substances play in her life (which is often to shield her from the pain of her own failures), the extent to which her rehabilitation is dependent upon successful treatment, and how they can help.

When Adoption Is the Permanent Plan

If reasonable efforts toward reunification have been made but were unsuccessful, or if there is compelling evidence that proceeding with reunification is not in the best interest of the children, the agency may instigate TPR and plan for adoption of the children. Sometimes relatives who are already caring for the children may adopt (as described above), the adoption may be a continuation of a nonrelative foster family care arrangement, or a new adoptive family may be found, necessitating another move for the child. If it appeared doubtful from the beginning that reunification would be successful, the worker and mother may have engaged in concurrent planning to speed up the TPR and adoption processes so the child will not be left in limbo for an extended period of time.

Of all permanency options, adoption is probably felt by the mother to be the biggest failure and involves the biggest adjustment for the children, particularly if it is a nonrelative adoption. Thus mother, children, and the adoptive family have special needs when adoption is the plan.

The mother's needs include the following:

- The mother has certain procedural rights, and the worker must ensure that these are protected throughout any planning toward adoption.

- When the plan is adoption, the mother has given up an important life role. With primary caregiving removed as an incentive, she may be less motivated to participate in rehabilitation programs and more vulnerable to recidivism and substance involvement. Typically, birth parents are forgotten when adoption is the plan. Yet resolving the mother's feelings around TPR and adoption may be important to her survival in the prison or community, carving out a meaningful life for herself, and being available to the children in a positive way when she does have contact with them again, either through an open adoption arrangement or when they become adults and search for her.

- Adoptive families vary in their views about openness of adoption, and when incarceration is involved, they may be particularly reluctant to allow the mother to become involved with their family. The mother may not understand this, and if openness cannot be negotiated she may need help in accepting it. On the other hand, if openness is the plan, she may need ongoing help and support in learning a new way to "parent" that does not involve provision of day-to-day care.

The child's needs include the following:

- For the child, moving from foster care to adoption, even if it is a continuation of the same living arrangement, is a big leap. As with any adoption, the child will need age-appropriate help in processing this information, understanding what adoption is and what it means in relation to the birth parent.

- The child needs a cover story to help him or her explain to others about the adoption and to handle simply and factually any questions about the birth parents.

- The child must revise his or her identity, since questions about "Who is my family" are also about "Who am I?" Such questions are not answered for a child only once. Rather, they reappear at each developmental stage in a different form, so the child is constantly reworking the answers. When parental incarceration is involved, the child will need special help creating a positive identity. Thus, the child's need for postadoptive treatment may be intermittent and life-long.

The adoptive family's needs include the following:

- The adoptive parents need to understand the importance of helping the child view their birth parent positively. It may be difficult, given the trauma and hurt that the birth parent may have caused the child and the departure from social norms of the parent's behavior. Most adoptive parents could use help in knowing how to talk about the parent to the child in a way that is both honest and positive, as well as how to answer specific questions the child might ask in an age-appropriate manner.

- The adoptive parent needs honest information about the child and his or her strengths and problems, help in understanding possible treatment needs, and where to find treatment resources.

- The adoptive parents need to understand that the child's problems are a reaction to what he or she has experienced. The adoptive parent must not see the child as a "bad seed" and every behavioral or emotional problem as confirmation of the child's unworthiness or likeness to the incarcerated parent.

- The adoptive parents may need help in evaluating openness of the adoption. They may have special fears related to the birth parent's criminality, fears around contamination of the child or danger to themselves or the child, and these need to be evaluated realistically, based upon the birth parent's actual situation rather than upon stereotypes of incarcerated women.

- If open adoption is the plan, the adoptive parents may need help in knowing how to include the birth parent, how to handle her involvement, and how to help the child understand and benefit from her involvement. If the parent remains incarcerated, this will involve a long-term commitment to involvement with the correctional system and with the parent within that system.

Practice Tips

While child welfare's focus is on the safety, permanency, and well-being of children, this is achieved primarily through supporting the child's caregiver(s), whether that be the birth parent, relatives, or adoptive parents. The following suggestions will help the worker support the child and his or her family in whatever permanent arrangement is chosen.

- Use your contacts in the prison to keep track of the incarcerated parent, particularly when she may move to another facility or is ready for discharge. Otherwise, she may be returned to the community without an adequate plan for her children.

- If the mother will be reentering the community, coordinate with pardon and parole and know the conditions of her parole so you can work together in a coordinated fashion.
  — Have the mother sign a release so you can contact her parole officer.
  — Help her be realistic about her difficulties, needs, and resources.
  — Run through likely scenarios and rehearse responses so she'll be prepared for situations that may arise, particularly concerning friends who may be involved in crime.
  — Help her develop appropriate help-seeking behaviors so she will know how and where to seek assistance before she gets into serious trouble.
  — Ensure she follows through with treatment referrals regarding substance use and help her develop a "safety net" to notice and intervene quickly if she has problems.

- If the plan is reunification, be specific about the details before the mother leaves prison.
  — Specify projected timelines for her to establish herself in the community before the child is returned.
  — Specify what you and she will accept as evidence that she is ready to provide a safe and stable home for her child.
  — Specify how you and she will coordinate with pardon and parole to ensure that she is able to meet the conditions of both systems and what she will do if she is in danger of violating the conditions of either.
  — Be aware of any special treatment programs that might support her efforts toward reunification, such as substance abuse programs that allow mother and child to live together in a supervised setting.
  — Help the mother deal with unrealistic ideas about reunification and how her children will relate to her so that disappointment doesn't become a demotivator.

- When kinship care is the permanent plan, help the family deal with the dynamics of their ongoing relationship as well as meeting physical needs.

— Help them develop a positive view of the mother and communicate that to the child, finding language they are comfortable with that includes the ideas that she loves the child, has had a hard life herself, and would want the child if she were able to care for him or her. In addition, help them be able to listen to the child's possible anger and resentment toward the parent, expressing empathy with the child and understanding of the feelings expressed without agreeing that the mother is "bad."

— Help them negotiate the parent's involvement, including physical presence, nurturing, and involvement in decision-making. Look to some of the newer models of practice, such as family conferencing and dispute resolution, for techniques.

— Discuss various options of providing long-term care for the child, including guardianship, foster care, and adoption, and the benefits or disadvantages of each. Look particularly at the financial consequence for the family of each arrangement.

• When adoption is the plan, the largest issue may be the openness of the adoption. Both birth parent and adoptive parent may have very strong feelings about this, and the issues will be different if the incarcerated parent is returning to the community or if an extended period of incarceration is expected. The focus of discussions must be around the needs of the child and how openness may contribute to his or her safety, permanency, and well-being.

— Regardless of the permanent arrangement, the child's needs are the primary consideration.

• Communicating with the child is absolutely essential, as secrecy leaves a child feeling anxious and needing to rely upon his or her own fantasy rather than real information. Not only should a child be informed about developments, but involved in decision-making as much as possible. Though each situation will be unique, cardinal rules for communicating with the child include:

— be simple and factual, finding nonpunitive language for giving information;

— avoid over-answering a child's questions by going too far beyond the intent of the question; allow the child to ask for more if he or she chooses;

— keep a finger on the child's anxiety pulse so you know when you have said something disturbing or have provided too much information for one dose;

— don't over-promise during decision-making, leaving the child to believe that his or her wants will be the deciding factor;

— end every conversation with a statement that invites the child for further conversations as he or she feels the need; and

— understand that children sometime request information indirectly through their behavior rather than directly with language.

- Regardless of the permanent arrangement, child safety is a paramount concern, and ongoing monitoring will be needed for a period of time.

- Ensure that the caregivers understand the treatment needs of the child, that these needs may be ongoing throughout the child's developmental stages, and how to get the treatment so needed.

Acknowledgments

Many people contributed time, energy, and ideas to the development of this handbook. The authors are especially grateful to Pamela Covington Katz and Madelyn DeWoody Freundlich for helping with the initial vision and outline of the handbook; to Peter Breen, Candace LaRue, Martha Raimon, and Evelyn Van Gelder for offering their expertise and experience during the review process; and to CWLA staff members Lynda Arnold, Kathy Barbell, Michael Petit, Mattie Satterfield, and Peggy Tierney for providing assistance and ongoing encouragement throughout this project.

Most importantly, the Child Welfare League of America wishes to thank Sybil Hite, Barbara Greenberg, and The Hite Foundation for their patience, support, and continuing commitment to children and families separated by incarceration.

References

Beck, A., Gilliard, D., Greenfeld, L. Harlow, C., Hester, T., Jankowski, L., Snell, T., Stephan, J., & Morton, D. (1992). *Survey of state prison inmates, 1991.* Washington, DC: U.S. Department of Justice, Office of Justice Programs, Bureau of Justice Statistics.

Beckerman, A. (1994). Mothers in prison: Meeting the prerequisite conditions for permanency planning. *Social Work, 39,* 9–14.

Beckerman, A. (1998). Charting a course: Meeting the challenge of permanency planning for children with incarcerated mothers. *Child Welfare, 77,* 513–529.

Block, K. J. & Potthast, M. J. (1998). Girl Scouts beyond bars: Facilitating parent-child contact in correctional settings. *Child Welfare, 77,* 561–578.

Bloom, B. (1995). Imprisoned mothers. In K. Gabel & D. Johnston (Eds.), *Children of incarcerated parents* (pp. 21–30). New York: Lexington Books.

Bloom, B. & Steinhart, D. (1993). *Why punish the children? A reappraisal of the children of incarcerated mothers in America.* San Francisco: National Council on Crime and Delinquency.

Brooks, J. & Bahna, K. (1994). "It's a family affair"—The incarceration of the American family: Confronting legal and social issues. 28 U.S.F.F. Rev. 271.

Bureau of Justice Statistics (1998). *Criminal offenders statistics.* Washington, DC: U.S. Department of Justice, Office of Justice Programs, Bureau of Justice Statistics.

Carlson, Bonnie E. (1996). Children of battered women: Research, programs, and services. In A. R. Roberts (Ed.), *Helping Battered Women* (pp.). New York: Oxford University Press.

Cassel, R. N. & VanVorst, R. B. (1961). Psychological needs of women in a correctional institution. *American Journal of Corrections, 23,* 22–24.

Centerforce (1999). *Annual report to the legislature regarding prison visitor services.* San Quentin, CA: Author.

Child Welfare League of America. (1998). *State agency survey on children with incarcerated parents.* Washington, DC: Author.

References

Conly, C. (1998). *The Women's Prison Association: Supporting women offenders and their families.* Washington, DC: U.S. Department of Justice, Office of Justice Programs, National Institute of Justice.

Genty, P. M. (1995). Termination of parental rights among prisoners. In K. Gabel & D. Johnston (Eds.), *Children of incarcerated parents* (pp. 167–182). New York: Lexington Books.

Genty, P. (1998). Permanency planning in the context of parental incarceration: Legal issues and recommendations. *Child Welfare, 77,* 543–559.

Gabel, K. & Girard K. (1995). Long term care nurseries in prison: A descriptive study. In K. Gabel & D. Johnston (Eds.), *Children of incarcerated parents* (pp. 237–254). New York: Lexington Books.

Gabel, S. (1992). Children of incarcerated and criminal parents: Adjustment, behavior, and prognosis. *Bulletin of the American Academy of Psychiatry Law, 20,* 33–45.

Gaudin, J. N. & Sutpen, R. (1993). Foster care vs. extended family care for children of incarcerated mothers. *Journal of Offender Rehabilitation, 19,* 129–147.

Gilliard, D. K. & Beck, A. J. (1998). *Bureau of Justice statistics bulletin: Prisoners in 1997.* Washington, DC: U.S. Department of Justice, Office of Justice Programs, Bureau of Justice Statistics.

Gilliard, D. K & Mumola, C. J. (1999). *Bureau of Justice statistics bulletin: Prisoners in 1998.* Washington, DC: U.S. Department of Justice, Office of Justice Programs, Bureau of Justice Statistics.

Greenfeld, L. & Snell, T. (1999). *Bureau of Justice statistics special report: Women offenders.* Washington, DC: U.S. Department of Justice, Office of Justice Programs.

Hairston, C. F. (1998). The forgotten parent: Understanding the factors that influence incarcerated fathers' relationships with their children. *Child Welfare, 77,* 617–639.

Hairston, C. F. (1999). Kinship care when parents are incarcerated. In J. P. Gleeson & C. F. Hairston (Eds.), *Kinship care: Improving practice through research* (pp. 189–211). Washington, DC: CWLA Press.

Hannon, G., Martin D., & Martin, M. (1984). Incarceration in the family: Adjustment of change. *Family Therapy, 11,* 253–260.

Harlow, C. W. (1998). *Profile of jail inmates 1996.* Washington, DC: U.S. Department of Justice.

Henriques, Z. M. (1982). *Imprisoned mothers and their children.* Washington, DC: University Press of America.

Henriques, Z. M. (1996). Imprisoned mothers and their children: Separation-reunion syndrome dual impact. *Women & Criminal Justice, 8,* 77–95.

Hostetter, E. C. & Jinnah, D. T. (1993). *Families of adult prisoners.* Prison Fellowship Ministries. [On-line]. Available: www.fcnetwork.org.

Hungerford, G. P. (1998). Caregivers of children whose mothers are incarcerated: A study of the kinship placement system. *Children Today, 24,* 23–27.

Johnston, D. (1992). *Report no. 6: Children of offenders.* Pasadena, CA: The Center for Children of Incarcerated Parents.

Johnston, D. (1995). The care and placement of prisoners' children. In K. Gabel & D. Johnston (Eds.), *Children of incarcerated parents* (pp. 103–123). New York: Lexington Books.

Johnston, D. (1995). Jailed mothers. In K. Gabel & D. Johnston (Eds.), *Children of incarcerated parents* (pp. 41–55). New York: Lexington Books.

Johnston, D. (1995). Effects of parental incarceration. In K. Gabel & D. Johnston (Eds.), *Children of incarcerated parents* (pp. 59–88). New York: Lexington Books.

Johnston, D. (1995). Parent-child visitation in the jail or prison. In K. Gabel & D. Johnston (Eds.), *Children of incarcerated parents* (pp. 135–143). New York: Lexington Books.

Johnston, D. & Gabel, K. (1995) Incarcerated parents. In K. Gabel & D. Johnston (Eds.), *Children of incarcerated parents* (pp. 3–20). New York: Lexington Books.

Johnston, D. & Carlin, M. (1996). Enduring trauma among children of criminal offenders. *Progress: Family Systems Research and Therapy, 5,* 9–36.

Kampfner, C. (1995). Post-traumatic stress reactions in children of imprisoned mothers. In K. Gabel & D. Johnston (Eds.), *Children of incarcerated parents* (pp. 89–100). New York: Lexington Books.

Katz, P. (1998). Supporting families and children of mothers in jail: An integrated child welfare and criminal justice strategy. *Child Welfare, 77,* 495–511.

McGowan, B. & Blumenthal, K. (1978). *Why punish the children? A study of women prisoners.* Hackensack, NJ: National Council on Crime and Delinquency.

Morash, M., Bynum, T. S., & Koons, B. A. (1998). Women offenders: Programming needs and promising approaches. *National Institute of Justice Research in Brief.* Washington, DC: U.S. Department of Justice, Office of Justice Programs, National Institute of Justice.

Mumola, C. (1999). *Bureau of Justice statistics special report: Substance abuse treatment, state and federal prisoners, 1997.* Washington, DC: U.S. Department of Justice, Office of Justice Programs.

National Clearinghouse on Child Abuse and Neglect. (1997). Termination of parental rights: Grounds for termination. In *Child abuse and neglect state statutes: Vol. 6. Permanency planning* (pp. 1–91). Washington, DC: Author.

Norman, J. A. (1995). Children of prisoners in foster care. In K. Gabel & D. Johnston (Eds.), *Children of incarcerated parents* (pp. 124–134). New York: Lexington Books.

The Osborne Association. (1993). How can I help? Working with children of incarcerated parents. In *Serving special children* (Vol. 1). New York: Author.

Philips, S. & Bloom, B. (1998). In whose best interest? The impact of changing public policy on relatives caring for children with incarcerated parents. *Child Welfare, 77,* 531–41.

Poe, L. (1995). A program for grandparent caregivers. In K. Gabel & D. Johnston (Eds.), *Children of incarcerated parents* (pp. 265–267). New York: Lexington Books.

Sametz, L. (1980, July). Children of incarcerated women. *Social Work,* 298–303.

Snell, T. S. & Morton, D. C. (1994). *Bureau of Justice special report: Women in prison* (NCJ-145321). Washington, DC: U.S. Department of Justice, Office of Justice Programs, Bureau of Justice Statistics.

Seymour, C. (1998). Children with parents in prison: Child welfare policy, program, and practice issues. *Child Welfare, 77,* 469–491.

Smith, B. & Elstein, S. G. (1994). *Children on hold: Improving the response to children whose parents are arrested and incarcerated.* Washington, DC: U.S. Department of Health and Human Services.

References

Stanton, S. (1980). *When mothers go to jail.* Lexington, MA: D.C. Health.

Ward, D. & Kassebaum, G. (1965). *Women's prison: Sex and social structure.* Chicago: Aldine.

Watson, P. S. & McAninch, W. S. (1997). *Guide to South Carolina criminal law and procedure* (5th ed.). Columbia: University of South Carolina Press.

Watterson, K. (1976). *Women in prison: Inside the concrete womb.* Boston: Northeastern Univ. Press.

Weilerstein, R. (1995). The prison MATCH program. In K. Gabel & D. Johnston (Eds.), *Children of incarcerated parents* (pp. 255–264). New York: Lexington Books.

Women's Prison Association. (1996). *When a mother is arrested: How the criminal justice and child welfare systems can work together more effectively.* Baltimore: Maryland Department of Human Resources.

Zalba, S. R. (1964). *Women prisoners and their families.* Sacramento, CA: Delmar.

Handbook Appendices

I.   Fact Sheet

II. Guide to Criminal Justice System

III. Additional Resources

    A. Information about the Criminal Justice System

    B. Information about Contacting Prisons and Locating Prisoners

    C. Information about Programs for Incarcerated Parents, their Children, and Families

    D. Information about Legal Issues

    E. Information for Specific Audiences
       1. Children with Incarcerated Parents
       2. Incarcerated Parents
       3. Caregivers of Children with Incarcerated Parents
       4. Service Providers, Volunteers and Other Advocates

    F. Information about Collaboration Between CJS and CWA

I. Fact Sheet

Children with Incarcerated Parents

I. Prisoners

- More than 1.8 million people are currently incarcerated in our nation's prisons and jails.[1]
- Since 1990, the number of incarcerated individuals has grown by nearly 676,700, an annual increase of 6.0%.[2]
- At the end of 1998, one in every 149 U.S. residents was incarcerated.[3]
- More than half of state and federal prison inmates are between the ages of 18-34.[4]
- In 1997, 47.9% of state and federal prisoners were white, 49.4% were black, 1.8% were American Indian/Alaska Native, and .8% were Asian/Pacific Islander. Hispanic inmates totaled an estimated 213,100 at yearend 1997.[5]
- At the end of 1998, state prisons operated at between 13% and 22% above capacity and federal prisons at 27% above capacity.[6]
- Approximately 3.8 million people in this country are on probation or parole.[7]

II. Women in Prison

- At the end of 1998, 84,427 women were under the jurisdiction of state or federal correctional authorities.[8]
- At midyear 1998, 63,791 women were held in local jails.[9]
- The number of women held in local jails has tripled since 1985.[10]
- Since 1990, the number of women inmates has grown at an average annual rate of 8.5% and has increased 92%.[11]
- In 1998, an estimated 3.2 million women in this country were arrested.[12]
- In 1998, an estimated 950,000 women were under the care, custody or control of correctional agencies—with 85% being supervised in the community by probation or parole agencies.[13]

A. Family Characteristics and Background

- The typical female offender comes from a single-parent home in which other family members have been incarcerated. One in five has lived in a family foster home or group care facility while growing up.[14]
- Nearly 6 in 10 women in state prison report having experienced physical or sexual abuse in the past, and for many, the abuse occurred before age 18.[15]
- Most women in prison have limited education and poor employment skills, and less than half have completed high school.[16]

B. Incarcerated Women and Drugs

- In 1996, more than 1/3 of female offenders were serving time for drug-related offenses.[17]
- From 1990-1996, the number of women incarcerated for drug-related offenses doubled.[18]
- Sixty-five percent of women in prison report having used drugs regularly.[19]
- Nearly 1 in 3 women serving time in state prisons report committing their offense to get money to buy drugs.[20]
- More than half the women in prison report committing their offense under the influence of drugs or alcohol.[21]

C. Incarcerated Mothers

- Approximately 75% of incarcerated women are mothers and two-thirds have children under age 18.[22]
- Seventy-two percent of women prisoners with children under age 18 lived with those children before entering prison.[23]
- Six percent of women entering prison are pregnant.[24]

III. Men in Prison

- At the end of 1998, there were more than 1.2 million men incarcerated in state and federal prisons.[25]
- Since 1990, the number of male inmates has increased at an average annual rate of 6.6%.[26]

A. Family Characteristics and Background

- The typical male inmate grew up in a single parent home and has at least one family member who has been incarcerated. More than 1/3 have experienced the incarceration of an immediate family member.[27]
- One in seven were raised by relatives, and 17% spent time in out-of-home care.[28]
- Thirty percent experienced parental substance abuse, and 12% report that they were physically or sexually abused in childhood.[29]
- Most male offenders have limited education and poor employment skills. At the time of their arrest, 90% had an income below $25,000 and 69% had an income below poverty level.[30]

B. Incarcerated Fathers

- Approximately 55% of incarcerated men are fathers of children under the age of 18.[31]
- Thirty-two percent of men in prison have two or more children under the age of 18.[32]
- On any given day, there are more than 500,000 fathers in prison.[33]

IV. Children with Parents in Prison

No one knows for certain how many children in this country have an incarcerated parent. Estimates suggest, though, that nearly 200,000 children under age 18 have an imprisoned mother and more than 1.7 million have an imprisoned father.[34] With the nation's incarcerated population growing at a rate of 6.0% annually,[35] the number of children with parents in prison will likely continue to increase.

A. Children with Incarcerated Fathers

- Ninety percent of children with incarcerated fathers are living with their mothers.[36]
- Ten percent are living with grandparents.[37]
- Three percent are living with relatives or other friends.[38]
- Two percent are living in a foster home or institution.[39]

B. Children with Incarcerated Mothers

- More than half of children with incarcerated mothers are living with their grandparents.[40]
- One quarter are living with other relatives or friends.[41]
- One quarter are living with their fathers.[42]
- Ten percent are living in a foster home or institution.[43]

C. Children with Incarcerated Parents and the Child Welfare System

- Approximately 10% of the children of female prisoners and 2% of the children of male prisoners are in some form of out-of-home care.[44]
- We don't know how many of these children were already in the child welfare system when their parents became incarcerated—and how many entered the system specifically because no one was able to care for them when their parents were incarcerated.

---

[1] Gilliard & Mumola, "Prisoners in 1998," *Bureau of Justice Statistics Bulletin.* (Washington, DC: U.S. Department of Justice, August 1999).

[2] Gilliard & Mumola.

[3] Gilliard & Mumola.

[4] Gilliard & Mumola.

[5] Gilliard & Mumola.

[6] Gilliard & Mumola.

[7] Correctional Populations in the United States,1995, *Bureau of Justice Statistics Bulletin*. (Washington, DC: U.S. Department of Justice, June 1997).

[8] Gilliard & Mumola.

[9] D. Gilliard, "Prison and Jail Inmates at Midyear 1998," *Bureau of Justice Statistics Bulletin*. (Washington, DC: U.S. Department of Justice, March 1999).

[10] Gilliard, 1999.

[11] Gilliard & Mumola.

[12] L. Greenfeld, "Women Offenders," *Bureau of Justice Statistics Special Report*. (Washington, DC: U.S. Department of Justice, December 1999).

[13] Greenfeld.

[14] D. Johnston, "Incarcerated Parents," in K. Gabel and D. Johnston (Eds.), *Children of Incarcerated Parents*. (Pasadena, California: Pacific Oaks Center for Children of Incarcerated Parents, 1995), pp.3–20.

[15] Greenfeld.

[16] D. Johnston, "Incarcerated Parents."

[17] D. Gilliard & A. Beck, "Prisoners in 1997," *Bureau of Justice Statistics Bulletin*. (Washington, DC: US Department of Justice, August 1998).

[18] Gilliard & Beck.

[19] T. Snell, "Women in Prison," *Bureau of Justice Statistics Special Report*. (Washington, DC: U.S. Department of Justice, 1992).

[20] Greenfeld.

[21] Greenfeld.

[22] Snell.

[23] Snell.

[24] Beck et al, "Survey of State Prison Inmates, 1991," *Bureau of Justice Statistics*. (Washington, DC: U.S. Department of Justice, 1992), p.10.

[25] Gilliard & Mumola.

[26] Gilliard & Mumola.

[27] D. Johnston, "Incarcerated Parents."

[28] D. Johnston, "Incarcerated Parents."

[29] D. Johnston, "Incarcerated Parents."

[30] D. Johnston, "Incarcerated Parents."

[31] Beck et al. (1992).

[32] Beck et al. (1992).

[33] C. F. Hairston, "Fathers in Prison," in K. Gabel & D. Johnston (Eds.), *Children of Incarcerated Parents*. (Pasadena, CA: Pacific Oaks Center for Children of Incarcerated Parents, 1995), pp.31–40.

[34] Gilliard & Mumola.

[35] Gilliard & Mumola.

[36] Beck et al., (1992).

[37] Beck et al., (1992).

[38] Beck et al., (1992).

[39] Beck et al., (1992).

[40] Beck et al., (1992).

[41] Beck et al., (1992).

[42] Beck et al., (1992).

[43] Beck et al., (1992).

[44] Beck et al., (1992).

II. Guide to Criminal Justice System

Figure 1. **What is the sequence of events in the criminal justice system?**

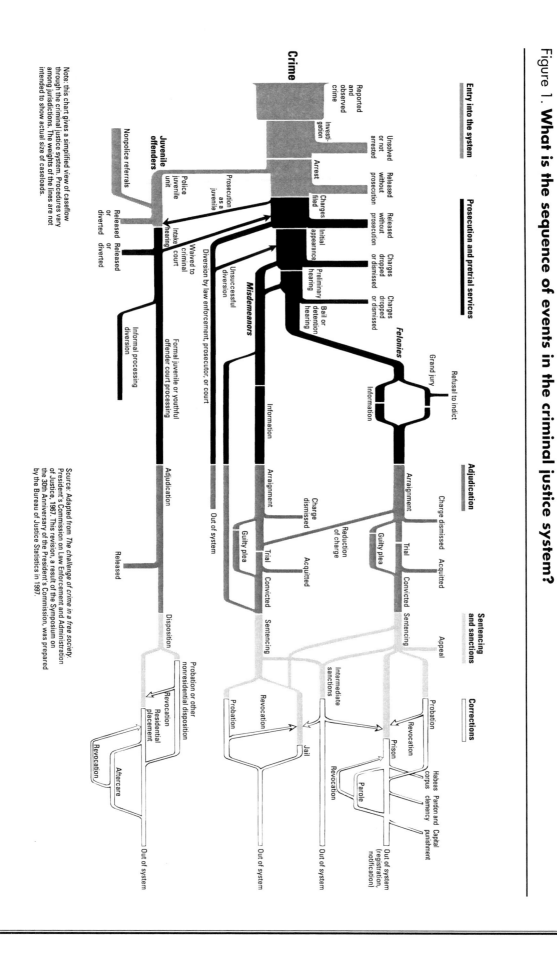

Note: this chart gives a simplified view of caseflow through the criminal justice system. Procedures vary among jurisdictions. The weights of the lines are not intended to show actual size of caseloads.

Source: Adapted from *The challenge of crime in a free society*, President's Commission on Law Enforcement and Administration of Justice, 1967. This revision, a result of the Symposium on the 30th Anniversary of the President's Commission, was prepared by the Bureau of Justice Statistics in 1997.

What is the sequence of events in the criminal justice system?

The private sector initiates the response to crime

This first response may come from individuals, families, neighborhood associations, business, industry, agriculture, educational institutions, the news media, or any other private service to the public.

It involves crime prevention as well as participation in the criminal justice process once a crime has been committed. Private crime prevention is more than providing private security or burglar alarms or participating in neighborhood watch. It also includes a commitment to stop criminal behavior by not engaging in it or condoning it when it is committed by others.

Citizens take part directly in the criminal justice process by reporting crime to the police, by being a reliable participant (for example, a witness or a juror) in a criminal proceeding and by accepting the disposition of the system as just or reasonable. As voters and taxpayers, citizens also participate in criminal justice through the policymaking process that affects how the criminal justice process operates, the resources available to it, and its goals and objectives. At every stage of the process from the original formulation of objectives to the decision about where to locate jails and prisons to the reintegration of inmates into society, the private

sector has a role to play. Without such involvement, the criminal justice process cannot serve the citizens it is intended to protect.

The response to crime and public safety involves many agencies and services

Many of the services needed to prevent crime and make neighborhoods safe are supplied by noncriminal justice agencies, including agencies with primary concern for public health, education, welfare, public works, and housing. Individual citizens as well as public and private agencies and organizations have joined with criminal justice agencies to prevent crime and make neighborhoods safe.

The description of the criminal and juvenile justice systems that follows portrays the most common sequence of events in response to serious criminal behavior.

Entry into the system

The justice system does not respond to most crime because so much crime is not discovered or reported to the police. Law enforcement agencies learn about crime from the reports of victims or other citizens, from discovery by a police officer in the field, from informants, or from investigative and intelligence work.

Once a law enforcement agency has established that a crime has been committed, a suspect must be identified and apprehended for the case to proceed through the system. Sometimes, a suspect is apprehended at the scene; however, identification of a suspect sometimes requires an

extensive investigation. Often, no one is identified or apprehended. In some instances, a suspect is arrested and later the police determine that no crime was committed and the suspect is released.

Prosecution and pretrial services

After an arrest, law enforcement agencies present information about the case and about the accused to the prosecutor, who will decide if formal charges will be filed with the court. If no charges are filed, the accused must be released. The prosecutor can also drop charges after making efforts to prosecute (nolle prosequi).

A suspect charged with a crime must be taken before a judge or magistrate without unnecessary delay. At the initial appearance, the judge or magistrate informs the accused of the charges and decides whether there is probable cause to detain the accused person. If the offense is not very serious, the determination of guilt and assessment of a penalty may also occur at this stage.

Often, the defense counsel is also assigned at the initial appearance. All suspects prosecuted for serious crimes have a right to be represented by an attorney. If the court determines the suspect is indigent and cannot afford such

representation, the court will assign counsel at the public's expense.

A pretrial-release decision may be made at the initial appearance, but may occur at other hearings or may be changed at another time during the process. Pretrial release and bail were traditionally intended to ensure appearance at trial. However, many jurisdictions permit pretrial detention of defendants accused of serious offenses and deemed to be dangerous to prevent them from committing crimes prior to trial.

The court often bases its pretrial decision on information about the defendant's drug use, as well as residence, employment, and family ties. The court may decide to release the accused on his/her own recognizance or into the custody of a third party after the posting of a financial bond or on the promise of satisfying certain conditions such as taking periodic drug tests to ensure drug abstinence.

In many jurisdictions, the initial appearance may be followed by a preliminary hearing. The main function of this hearing is to discover if there is probable cause to believe that the accused committed a known crime within the jurisdiction of the court. If the judge does not find probable cause, the case is dismissed; however, if the judge or magistrate finds

The response to crime and public safety involves many agencies and services

There is no single criminal justice system in this country. We have many similar systems that are individually unique. Criminal cases may be handled differently in different jurisdictions, but court decisions based on the due process guarantees of the U.S. Constitution require that specific steps be taken in the administration of criminal justice so that the individual will be protected from undue intervention from the State.

Criminal cases are brought by the government through the criminal justice system

We apprehend, try, and punish offenders by means of a loose confederation of agencies at all levels of government. Our American system of justice has evolved from the English common law into a complex series of procedures and decisions. Founded on the concept that crimes against an individual are crimes against the State, our justice system prosecutes individuals as though they victimized all of society. However, crime victims are involved throughout the process and many justice agencies have programs which focus on helping victims.

What is the sequence of events in the criminal justice system? *(continued)*

probable cause for such a belief, or the accused waives his or her right to a preliminary hearing, the case may be bound over to a grand jury.

A grand jury hears evidence against the accused presented by the prosecutor and decides if there is sufficient evidence to cause the accused to be brought to trial. If the grand jury finds sufficient evidence, it submits to the court an indictment, a written statement of the essential facts of the offense charged against the accused.

Where the grand jury system is used, the grand jury may also investigate criminal activity generally and issue indictments called grand jury originals that initiate criminal cases. These investigations and indictments are often used in drug and conspiracy cases that involve complex organizations. After such an indictment, law enforcement tries to apprehend and arrest the suspects named in the indictment.

Misdemeanor cases and some felony cases proceed by the issuance of an information, a formal, written accusation submitted to the court by a prosecutor. In some jurisdictions, indictments may be required in felony cases. However, the accused may choose to waive a grand jury indictment and, instead, accept service of an information for the crime.

In some jurisdictions, defendants, often those without prior criminal records, may be eligible for diversion from prosecution subject to the completion of specific conditions such as drug treatment. Successful completion of the conditions may result in the dropping of charges or the expunging of the criminal record where the defendant is required to plead guilty prior to the diversion.

Adjudication

Once an indictment or information has been filed with the trial court, the accused is scheduled for arraignment. At the arraignment, the accused is informed of the charges, advised of the rights of criminal defendants, and asked to enter a plea to the charges. Sometimes, a plea of guilty is the result of negotiations between the prosecutor and the defendant.

If the accused pleads guilty or pleads *nolo contendere* (accepts penalty without admitting guilt), the judge may accept or reject the plea. If the plea is accepted, no trial is held and the offender is sentenced at this proceeding or at a later date. The plea may be rejected and proceed to trial if, for example, the judge believes that the accused may have been coerced.

If the accused pleads not guilty or not guilty by reason of insanity, a date is set for the trial. A person accused of a serious crime is guaranteed a trial by jury. However, the accused may ask for a bench trial where the judge, rather than a jury, serves as the finder of fact. In both instances the prosecution and defense present evidence by questioning witnesses while the judge decides on issues of law. The trial results in acquittal or conviction on the original charges or on lesser included offenses.

After the trial a defendant may request appellate review of the conviction or sentence. In some cases, appeals of convictions are a matter of right; all States with the death penalty provide for automatic appeal of cases involving a death sentence. Appeals may be subject to the discretion of the appellate court and may be granted only on acceptance of a defendant's petition for a *writ of certiorari*. Prisoners may also appeal their sentences through civil rights petitions and *writs of habeas corpus* where they claim unlawful detention.

Sentencing and sanctions

After a conviction, sentence is imposed. In most cases the judge decides on the sentence, but in some jurisdictions the sentence is decided by the jury, particularly for capital offenses.

In arriving at an appropriate sentence, a sentencing hearing may be held at which evidence of aggravating or mitigating circumstances is considered. In assessing the circumstances surrounding a convicted person's criminal behavior, courts often rely on presentence investigations by probation agencies or other designated authorities. Courts may also consider victim impact statements.

The sentencing choices that may be available to judges and juries include one or more of the following:

• the death penalty
• incarceration in a prison, jail, or other confinement facility
• probation—allowing the convicted person to remain at liberty but subject to certain conditions and restrictions such as drug testing or drug treatment
• fines—primarily applied as penalties in minor offenses
• restitution—requiring the offender to pay compensation to the victim.

In some jurisdictions, offenders may be sentenced to alternatives to incarceration that are considered more severe than straight probation but less severe than a prison term. Examples of such sanctions include boot camps, intense supervision often with drug treatment and testing, house arrest and electronic monitoring, denial of Federal benefits, and community service.

In many jurisdictions, the law mandates that persons convicted of certain types of offenses serve a prison term. Most jurisdictions permit the judge to set the sentence length within certain limits, but some have determinate sentencing laws that stipulate a specific sentence length that must be served and cannot be altered by a parole board.

Corrections

Offenders sentenced to incarceration usually serve time in a local jail or a State prison. Offenders sentenced to less than 1 year generally go to jail; those sentenced to more than 1 year go to prison. Persons admitted to the Federal system or a State prison system may be held in prisons with varying levels of custody or in a community correctional facility.

A prisoner may become eligible for parole after serving a specific part of his or her sentence. Parole is the conditional release of a prisoner before the prisoner's full sentence has been served. The decision to grant parole is made by an authority such as a parole board, which has power to grant or revoke parole or to discharge a parolee altogether. The way parole decisions are made varies widely among jurisdictions.

Offenders may also be required to serve out their full sentences prior to release (expiration of term). Those sentenced under determinate sentencing laws can be released only after they have served their full sentence (mandatory release) less any "goodtime" received while in prison. Inmates get goodtime credits against their sentences automatically or by earning them through participation in programs.

If released by a parole board decision or by mandatory release, the releasee will be under the supervision of a parole officer in the community for the balance of his or her unexpired sentence. This supervision is governed by specific conditions of release, and the releasee may be returned to prison for violations of such conditions.

Recidivism

Once the suspects, defendants, or offenders are released from the jurisdiction of a criminal justice agency, they may be processed through the criminal justice system again for a new crime. Long term studies show that many suspects who are arrested have prior criminal histories and those with a greater number of prior arrests were more likely to be arrested again. As the courts take prior criminal history into account at sentencing, most prison inmates have a prior criminal history and many have been incarcerated before. Nationally, about half the inmates released from State prison will return to prison.

The juvenile justice system

Juvenile courts usually have jurisdiction over matters concerning children, including delinquency, neglect, and adoption. They also handle "status offenses" such as truancy and running away, which are not applicable to adults. State statutes define which persons are under the original jurisdiction of the juvenile court. The upper age of juvenile court jurisdiction is 17 in most States.

The processing of juvenile offenders is not entirely dissimilar to adult criminal processing, but there are crucial differences. Many juveniles are referred to juvenile courts by law enforcement officers, but many others are referred by school officials, social services agencies, neighbors, and even parents, for behavior or conditions that are determined to require intervention by the formal system for social control.

At arrest, a decision is made either to send the matter further into the justice system or to divert the case out of the system, often to alternative programs. Examples of alternative programs include drug treatment, individual or group counseling, or referral to educational and recreational programs.

When juveniles are referred to the juvenile courts, the court's intake department or the prosecuting attorney determines whether sufficient grounds exist to warrant filing a petition that requests an adjudicatory hearing or a request to transfer jurisdiction to criminal court. At this point, many juveniles are released or diverted to alternative programs.

All States allow juveniles to be tried as adults in criminal court under certain circumstances. In many States, the legislature *statutorily excludes* certain (usually serious) offenses from the jurisdiction of the juvenile court regardless of the age of the accused. In some States and at the Federal level under certain circumstances, prosecutors have the *discretion* to either file criminal charges against juveniles directly in criminal courts or proceed through the juvenile justice process. The juvenile court's intake department or the prosecutor may petition the juvenile court to *waive* jurisdiction to criminal court. The juvenile court also may order *referral* to criminal court for trial as adults. In some jurisdictions, juveniles processed as adults may upon conviction be sentenced to either an adult or a juvenile facility.

In those cases where the juvenile court retains jurisdiction, the case may be handled formally by filing a delinquency petition or informally by diverting the juvenile to other agencies or programs in lieu of further court processing.

If a petition for an adjudicatory hearing is accepted, the juvenile may be brought before a juvenile court quite unlike the court with jurisdiction over adult offenders. Despite the considerable discretion associated with juvenile court proceedings, juveniles are afforded many of the due-process safeguards associated with adult criminal trials. Several States permit the use of juries in juvenile courts; however, in light of the U.S. Supreme Court holding that juries are not essential to juvenile hearings, most States do not make provisions for juries in juvenile courts.

In disposing of cases, juvenile courts usually have far more discretion than adult courts. In addition to such options as probation, commitment to a residential facility, restitution, or fines, State laws grant juvenile courts the power to order removal of children from their homes to foster homes or treatment facilities. Juvenile courts also may order participation in special programs aimed at shoplifting prevention, drug counseling, or driver education.

Once a juvenile is under juvenile court disposition, the court may retain jurisdiction until the juvenile legally becomes an adult (at age 21 in most States). In some jurisdictions, juvenile offenders may be classified as youthful offenders which can lead to extended sentences.

Following release from an institution, juveniles are often ordered to a period of aftercare which is similar to parole supervision for adult offenders. Juvenile offenders who violate the conditions of aftercare may have their aftercare revoked, resulting in being recommitted to a facility. Juveniles who are classified as youthful offenders and violate the conditions of aftercare may be subject to adult sanctions.

The governmental response to crime is founded in the intergovernmental structure of the United States

Under our form of government, each State and the Federal Government has its own criminal justice system. All systems must respect the rights of individuals set forth in court interpretation of the U.S. Constitution and defined in case law.

State constitutions and laws define the criminal justice system within each State and delegate the authority and responsibility for criminal justice to various jurisdictions, officials, and institutions. State laws also define criminal behavior and groups of children or acts under jurisdiction of the juvenile courts.

Municipalities and counties further define their criminal justice systems through local ordinances that proscribe the local agencies responsible for

What is the sequence of events in the criminal justice system? (continued)

criminal justice processing that were not established by the State.

Congress has also established a criminal justice system at the Federal level to respond to Federal crimes such as bank robbery, kidnaping, and transporting stolen goods across State lines.

The response to crime is mainly a State and local function

Very few crimes are under exclusive Federal jurisdiction. The responsibility to respond to most crime rests with State and local governments. Police protection is primarily a function of cities and towns. Corrections is primarily a function of State governments. Most justice personnel are employed at the local level.

Discretion is exercised throughout the criminal justice system

Discretion is "an authority conferred by law to act in certain conditions or situations in accordance with an official's or an official agency's own considered judgment and conscience."[1] Discretion is exercised throughout the government. It is a part of decisionmaking in all government systems from mental health to education, as well as criminal justice. The limits of discretion vary from jurisdiction to jurisdiction.

Concerning crime and justice, legislative bodies have recognized that they cannot anticipate the range of circumstances surrounding each crime, anticipate local mores, and enact laws that clearly encompass all conduct that is criminal and all that is not.[2] Therefore, persons charged with the day-to-day response to crime are expected to exercise their own judgment within limits set by law. Basically, they must decide—

- whether to take action
- where the situation fits in the scheme of law, rules, and precedent
- which official response is appropriate.[3]

Who exercises discretion?

These criminal justice officials . . . . . . must often decide whether or not or how to—

Police	Enforce specific laws Investigate specific crimes Search people, vicinities, buildings Arrest or detain people
Prosecutors	File charges or petitions for adjudication Seek indictments Drop cases Reduce charges
Judges or magistrates	Set bail or conditions for release Accept pleas Determine delinquency Dismiss charges Impose sentence Revoke probation
Correctional officials	Assign to type of correctional facility Award privileges Punish for disciplinary infractions
Paroling authorities	Determine date and conditions of parole Revoke parole

To ensure that discretion is exercised responsibly, government authority is often delegated to professionals. Professionalism requires a minimum level of training and orientation, which guide officials in making decisions. The professionalism of policing is due largely to the desire to ensure the proper exercise of police discretion.

The limits of discretion vary from State to State and locality to locality. For example, some State judges have wide discretion in the type of sentence they may impose. In recent years other States have sought to limit the judge's discretion in sentencing by passing mandatory sentencing laws that require prison sentences for certain offenses.

Notes

[1] Roscoe Pound, "Discretion, dispensation and mitigation: The problem of the individual special case," New York University Law Review (1960) 35:925, 926.

[2] Wayne R. LaFave, Arrest: The decision to take a suspect into custody (Boston: Little, Brown & Co., 1964), p.63-184.

[3] Memorandum of June 21, 1977, from Mark Moore to James Vorenberg, "Some abstract notes on the issue of discretion."

III. Additional Resources

A. Information about the Criminal Justice System

- **National Criminal Justice Reference Center:** NCJRS provides a variety of criminal and juvenile justice information services including access to its document collection of more than 135,000 books, reports and articles. Visit online at www.ncjrs.org or call 800-851-3420.

- **Bureau of Justice Statistics:** BJS is a primary source for criminal justice statistics in the United States. BJS analyzes, publishes and disseminates data on all aspects of our criminal justice system. Contact BJS by writing to the Bureau of Justice Statistics, 810 Seventh Street, NW, Washington, DC 20531, or by calling 202-307-0765. Many BJS reports are available online at www.ojp.usdoj.gov/bjs.

- **The Sourcebook of Criminal Justice Statistics, 1998,** edited by Kathleen Maguire and Ann L. Pastore, is also available online at www.albany.edu/sourcebook.

- **American Correctional Association:** ACA is an umbrella organization of professionals representing many areas corrections & criminal justice, including federal, state, and military correctional facilities and prisons, county jails and detention centers, probation/parole agencies, and community corrections/ halfway houses. Contact ACA by writing to ACA, 4380 Forbes Boulevard, Lanham, MD, 20706-4322, or by calling (800) 222-5646, or by visiting online at www.corrections.com/aca.

B. Information about Contacting Prisons and Locating Prisoners

- ### Directories

  1999 Directory of Juvenile and Adult Correctional Departments, Institutions, Agencies and Paroling Authorities, April 1999, American Correctional Association, 800-222-5646, www.corrections.com/aca, includes names, addresses and fax/telephone numbers for wardens and administrators at more than 4000 state correctional institutions, also Personnel Locator to aid in locating staff.

- ### Federal Prisons

  Federal Bureau of Prisons, 320 First St., NW., Washington, DC 20534. For information, visit the website at www.bop.gov or call the Office of Public Affairs at 202-307-3198.

- ### State Prisons

  To contact your state's Department of Corrections, use the government pages in your phone book or visit www.corrections.com for links to states Departments of Corrections.

- ### Inmate Information

  Federal: For information about Federal inmates incarcerated from 1982 to the present, call the national Inmate Locator at 202-307-3126. You may also submit an email request for information through the Federal Bureau of Prisons website at www.bop.gov. For information about Federal inmates released before 1982, write to the Office of Communications and Archives, Federal Bureau of Prisons, 320 First St. NW, Washington, DC 20534, Attn: Historic Inmate Locator Request. Include as much identifying information as possible.

  State: Most state Departments of Corrections have their own locator systems. Contact your state Department of Corrections for specific information or access an online directory of links to state Departments of Corrections by visiting www.corrections.com/links/state.html.

C. Information about Programs for Incarcerated Parents, their Children and Families

Directory of Programs and Organizations

For a statewide listing of programs serving children and families of offenders, see the **Directory of Programs Serving Families of Adult Offenders,** edited by James W. Mustin, 1998, and available from the National Institute of Corrections, www.nicic.org, 800-877-1461 (provides an extensive state-by-state listing of programs and organizations focused on children and families of offenders).

Establishing a Program

For information about establishing a program in your community, contact the **Family and Corrections Network (FCN)** at (804)589-3036 or access the website at http:\\www.fcnetwork.org. FCN is a membership organization that provides information about programs serving families of offenders and offers consultation and technical assistance in program development.

Program Descriptions

Maternal Ties: A Selection of Programs for Female Offenders, Cynthia Blinn, Editor, 1997, American Correctional Association, 800-222-5646, provides descriptions of fourteen programs designed to help incarcerated mothers maintain ties with their children.

Parents in Prison: Addressing the Needs of Families, James Boudouris, Ph.D, 1996, American Correctional Association, 800-222-5646, also available through Amazon.com $22.95, provides information from a national survey of prison-based programs for incarcerated mothers and includes personal contacts in prison-based and community-based programs located in prisons across the country.

Program Standards

Federal Bureau of Prison's Parenting Program Standards (PS5355.03), January 20, 1995, www.bop.gov/progstat/53559993.html (includes sample statement of work).

Articles about Programs

- **Family Views in Correctional Programs,** Creasie Finney Hairston, Ph.D, Encyclopedia of Social Work. 19th Edition. Washington, DC. NASA Press (1995):991–996.

- **Parenting Programs for Imprisoned Mothers,** Irene Glasser, Practicing Anthropology, Vol. 14, No. 3, Summer 1992.

- **Family-Based Crime Prevention,** Lawrence W. Sherman, in Preventing Crime: What Works, What Doesn't, What's Promising, by University of Maryland, Department of Criminology and Criminal Justice, Office of Justice Programs Research Report, February 1997, NCJ 165366, Justice Information Center www.ncjrs.org.

D. Information about Legal Issues

1. Articles

"Permanency Planning in the Context of Parental Incarceration: Legal Issues and Recommendations," Philip Genty, CHILD WELFARE, September/October 1998, 543–559.

"Termination of Parental Rights Among Prisoners," Philip Genty, in Children of Incarcerated Parents, Katherine Gabel and Denise Johnston, Editors, New York: Lexington Books (1995) pp. 167–182.

"Meeting the Needs of Children of Incarcerated Parents," Ann Metcalf Craig, Child Law Practice, August, 1998, American Bar Association's Center on Children and the Law.

"'It's a Family Affair'—The Incarceration of the American Family: Confronting Legal and Social Issues," Justin Brooks and Kimberly Bahna, University of San Francisco Law Review, Winter, 1994, volume 28, page 271.

"Terminating Parental Rights of Incarcerated Parents," Carol Amadio and Rosemary Mulryan, Chicago Bar Association Record, February 1992.

"You Can Never Go Home Again: The Florida Legislature Adds Incarceration to the List of Statutory Grounds for Termination of Parental Rights," The Hon. Jean M Johnson and Christa N Flowers, Florida State University Law Review, 1998, volume 25, page 335.

2. Statutes

Many state statutes addressing termination of parental rights specifically provide that a parent's incarceration or felony conviction may be grounds for termination of parental rights (TPR). The statutes vary considerably though in terms of the accompanying factors that must be evaluated in addition to the incarceration itself. It is impossible to catalogue those variations here, and in addition state laws are subject to change at any time. In general, though, most statutes that include incarceration as possible grounds for TPR are tied to the length of the parent's sentence (eg. Idaho, Iowa, Colorado, Ohio, Tennessee, Texas); the parent's incapacity or failure to plan for the child (eg. Arkansas, California); the instability of the child's resultant placement (eg. Massachusetts, Missouri); the parent's unfitness to parent (eg. Arizona, Wyoming); the crime for which the parent was incarcerated and whether the crime victimized the child at issue, a sibling, or other child in the household (eg. Deleware, Maine, Iowa); or some combination of the previous factors (eg. Louisiana, New Hampshire, Ohio, Florida). (For the text of state TPR statutes, see National Clearinghouse on Child Abuse and Neglect, 1997 State Statute Series, Volume VI, Permanency Planning, p. 91).

To review a state by state compilation of statutory language providing for termination of parental rights, visit online the National Clearinghouse on Child Abuse and Neglect's State Statute Series at www.calib.com/nccanch/services/statutes.htm. Click on "Volume VI, Permanency Planning."

3. Selected Caselaw

Termination of Parental Rights

In re Sabrina N., (60 Cal. App. 4th 996, 1/13/98). Incarcerated father's petition for an Extraordinary Writ of Mandate following termination of his parental rights was granted by the California Court of Appeals. Noting that the prospect of reunification was "dim" based on the father's drug abuse, domestic violence, and failure to obtain medical care for the child prior to his incarceration, the court nonetheless found that the child welfare agency failed to provide the father with reasonable reunification services as required by law. The court noted that the agency must affirmatively offer services to an incarcerated parent, inform the prison of the parent's need for services, find out what services are available in the prison, and request that those services be provided to the parent. Citing the agency's failure to communicate with the father despite receiving three letters from the father, its failure to contact the prison, and its failure to provide any visitation required by the case plan, the court found the agency failed to make reasonable efforts and ordered the trial court to reexamine the case.

*In re Angel R., 965 Cal. Rptr. 2d 311 (Ct. App. 1998). Child welfare agency offered adequate reunification services to incarcerated father because his own actions, which resulted in his out-of-state imprisonment, placed him beyond reach of any meaningful rehabilitation services; standard at permanency hearing is not whether services were best but whether they were reasonable under the circumstances.

Matter of Oneka O, (New York, 1st Dept., 5/4/98). Termination of incarcerated father's parental rights upheld where evidence showed he made only one phone call to the child welfare agency during a six month period to inquire about the possibility of visiting with his children, and the agency had made efforts to contact the father to discuss the children's placement. In addition, there was no evidence that the father tried to keep in contact with the children prior to his incarceration, or that the agency had discouraged visits.

In re Treadwell, (Mich. Ct. App., 10/24/95). Termination of incarcerated mother's parental rights upheld where mother sentenced to concurrent terms of five to fifteen years and her incarceration would deprive her children of a normal home for at least two years after the filing of the custody petition. Evidence supporting the decision included the mother's long term drug abuse, failure to complete drug treatment, failure to attend the majority of visits with her children, and failure to attend counseling.

*Michael J. v. Arizona Dep't of Econ. Sec., 1999 WL 92541 (Ariz. Ct. App.) Trial court failed to establish by clear and convincing evidence that father abandoned child; although father's incarceration hindered relationship with child, his efforts to discover child's whereabouts after child welfare agency failed to tell him and to establish visitation with child demonstrated his intent to form a relationship with his child.

*E.W.R. v. W.T.J., 702 So. 2d 1343 (Fla. Dist Ct. App. 1997). Even though father would be incarcerated for a long time, stepfather wanted to adopt child, and father had committed sexual crimes, his parental rights should not have been terminated on abandonment grounds, since his failure to provide financial support was due to his lack of income while incarcerated and child's mother interfered with his attempts to communicate with child.

---

* Reprinted with permission from the American Bar Association, Center on children and the Law. Copyright 1999, American Bar Association. All rights reserved. Original summaries appeared in "ABA Child Law Practice" (CLP), a monthly publication of the ABA Center on Children and the Law. CLP abstracts current state and federal case law each month, and includes practical articles for legal and other professionals in the child welfare field. For more information and for a free sample issue, contact Lisa M. Waxler, Subscription Specialist, at 202/662-1743.

Visitation

*In re CJ, 729 A.2d 89 (Pa. Super. Ct 1999). Limiting incarcerated parents' visitation with six dependant children to times when parents were transported to nearby prison for dependency review hearings was appropriate since transporting children to parents' remote prison locations would pose "grave threat" to children and it would not be in the children's best interest to endure long trips to visit parents because children had physical and/or emotional problems requiring close supervision. (ABA Center on Children and the Law, Child Law Practice, September 1999, p. 101).

*In re Dylan T., 76 Cal. Rptr.2d 684 (Ct. App. 1998). Court cannot deny visitation to incarcerated parent based solely on child's young age because state must show by clear and convincing evidence that visitation would be detrimental to child; child was one year and three months old when mother was jailed for six months after a substance abuse conviction.

*Green v. Department of Health and Rehab. Servs., 696 So. 2d 1351 (Fla. Dist. Ct. App. 1997). Incarcerated mother was not entitled to modification of visitation order entered in connection with dependency adjudication to allow her to have personal visits with son on a regular basis, since mother was unable to show material change in circumstances of that personal visitation was in child's best interest.

*Jonathan v. Orange County Social Servs. Agency, 62 Cal. Rptr. 208 (Ct. App. 1997). Fifty-mile geographical limitation on visitation component of reunification plan was arbitrarily applied to father incarcerated 275 miles away; statutory requirement that reunification services be provided to incarcerated parent "where appropriate" meant determining that services would not be detrimental to child and could not be based on geography alone.

Support

*Bendixon v. Bendixon, 962 P.2d 170 (Alaska 1998). Lower court improperly refused to reduce father's child support payments because his incarceration was equivalent to "voluntary unemployment;" while incarceration is a foreseeable consequence of voluntary criminal acts, it differs from voluntary unemployment in that jailed parent lacks potential job prospects or potential income.

*Rupp v. Grubb, 962 P.2d 1074 (Kan. 1998). Father was not entitled to abatement of child support payments because of his 15-year incarceration for drug-related felonies; incarceration, standing alone, is not a legal justification to modify or suspend a child support obligation, regardless of whether support order was made in a divorce or paternity proceeding.

*State v. Valentine, 1997 WL 251303 (Ariz. Ct. App.). Incarcerated father was denied right to a fair hearing when trial court failed to order department of corrections ot provide father access to the phone so he could participate in his child support hearing.

E. Information for Specific Audiences

1. Materials for Children with Incarcerated Parents

Books

All Kinds of Families, Norma Simon, October 1987, Albert Whitman & Co., available through Amazon.com, $10.47, ages 4–8.

Breaking Out, Barthe Declements, August 1993, Demco Media, Amazon.com: Out of Print (with reviews), seventh grader must adjust to his father's imprisonment, for older children.

Coping When a Parent Is in Jail, John J. La Valle, June 1995, Rosen Publishing Group, available through Amazon.com at $17.95.

Let's Talk About When Your Parent Is in Jail, Maureen Wittbold, August 1998, Powerkids Press, Amazon.com $15.93.

Queenie Peavy, Robert Burch, Viking Press, Amazon.com $3.99 (with reviews), ages 9–2.

A Visit to the Big House, Oliver Butterworth, Amazon.com: Out of Print (with review).

Into the Great Forest: A Story for Children Away from Parents for the First Time, Irene Wineman Marcus & Paul Marcus, Ph.D, 1992, New York: Magination Press, 800-374-2721.

The Kissing Hand, by Audrey Penn, 1993, Child Welfare League of America, a book for children temporarily separated from their loved ones, $16.95, 800-407-6723, www.cwla.org.

Zachary's New Home: A Story for Foster and Adopted Children, by Geraldine M. Blomquist, MSW, & Paul B. Blomquist, 1990, New York: Magination Press, 800-374-2721, www.maginationpress.com, age 3–8.

Workbooks

All About Change, Kathy Kagy-Taylor and Donna Dansker, 1991, The Aring Institute of Beech Acres, 6881 Beechmont Ave., Cincinnati, OH, 45230, (513) 231-6630, for children in grades K–4.

Because . . . Somebody Loves Me, Child Welfare League of America (1996), a workbook for children coping with painful transitions, helps them express feelings and come to terms with reality in a positive comforting way, to order, call 800-407-6723, $3.95 apiece.

Help for Kids! Understanding Your Feelings About Having a Parent in Prison or Jail (for Kids Ages Six and Older), by Carole Gesme, M.A., CCDP, with consultation from Michele Kopfmann. $9.95 for manual. To purchase: Carole Gesme, 4036 Kerry Court, Minnetonka, MN 55345, (612) 938-9163 (phone), (612) 935-2038 (fax).

If You Have a Parent in Jail Then this Book is For You, By Craig, Kevin, Josselyn, Alan, Brittney, with Bonnie Ayer and Amy Bigelow, School counselors at Flynn School, Burlington, VT, 05401 (1996).

Two in Every 100: A Special Workbook for Children with a Parent in Prison, published by Reconciliation Ministries, Inc., P.O. Box 90827, Nashville, TN, 37209, (615) 292-6371.

2. Materials for Incarcerated Parents

The Foster Care Handbook for Incarcerated Parents: A Manual of Your Legal Rights and Responsibilities, by the Inmate Foster Care Committee, The Children's Center, Bedford Hills Correctional Facility, Bedford Hills, NY, 10547, (914) 241-3100.

I Love You This Much, Pennsylvania Department of Education and Pennsylvania Department of Corrections, (1995), is a workbook designed to facilitate communication between incarcerated parents and their children. Prepared by women inmates in the State Correctional Institution at Muncy, Pennsylvania, this 164-page workbook includes games, activities, sample letters, and suggestions to help incarcerated men and women nurture their children from a distance and actively participate in parenting. To inquire about this workbook, contact Melinda Yowell, Parenting Director, State Correctional Institution at Muncy, P.O. Box 180, Muncy, PA 17756, (717) 546-3171.

Parenting from a Distance: Your Rights and Responsibilities, by Jan Walker, M.A., The Interstate Printers & Publishers, Inc., Danville, Illinois (1987), is not specific to incarcerated parents, but includes incarcerated parents as one example of parenting from a distance. Includes information about rights and responsibilities, telling children, daily routine, touching from a distance, visiting, holidays, the systems (including child welfare), shared parenting, and reunion. Also includes forms and sample letters (including letter to foster care caseworker from incarcerated parent) to help parents acquire and maintain information about their children.

Parenting from Inside/Out: The Voices of Mothers in Prison, edited by Kathy Boudin & Rozann Greco, The Children's Center, Bedford Hills Correctional Facility, Bedford Hills, NY, 10547, (914) 241-3100.

A Vision Beyond Survival: A Resource Guide for Incarcerated Women, 1995, National Women's Law Center, 11 Dupont Circle, NW, Suite 800, Washington, DC, 20036, (202) 588-5180, is written specifically for women in the DC/MD/VA area but contains general information that is helpful to all incarcerated women, including a section on child custody concerns.

Questions for Dad, by Dwight Twilley, 1994, Boston: Charles E. Tuttle Company, Inc., author describes in detail a creative method for parents and children living apart to communicate and enhance their long distance relationships.

3. Materials for Caregivers of Children with Incarcerated Parents

Manual for Grandparents-Relative Caregivers and their Advocates, Legal Services for Prisoners with Children, 100 McAllister, San Francisco, CA 94102, 415-255-7036.

Grandparent Caregivers: A National Guide, Legal Services for Prisoners with Children, 100 McAllister, San Francisco, CA 94102, 415-255-7036.

4. Materials for Service Providers, Volunteers and Other Advocates

Working with Children and Families

How Can I Help? A Three-Volume Series on Serving Special Children, Vol. I: Working with Children of Incarcerated Parents, Vol. II: Sustaining & Enhancing Family Ties, Vol. III: Resources for Supporting the Children of Incarcerated Parents, developed by the Osborne Association, 135 E. 15th St., New York, NY, 10003, (212) 673-6633, $10.00 per set (includes postage and handling).

Parenting from the Inside: Maintaining the Bond, by Maud MacArthur, B.A., and Theresa LaBarre, Psy.D., 1996, is the curriculum for the FCI and FPC Danbury Parenting Program. It includes a teacher's guide, a parent's manual, and sections on family literacy, parenting skills, and long distance parenting. For more information, contact FCI Danbury, Route 37, Danbury, Connecticut 06811-3099, 203-743-6471.

Homemade Books to Help Kids Cope: An Easy-to-Learn Technique for Parents and Professionals, by Robert G. Ziegler, M.D., 1992, New York: Magination Press, 800-374-2721.

Training Manual on Working with Women in the Criminal Justice System, developed by the Women's Justice Alliance, 1997, c/o Women's Prison Association, 110 Second Avenue, New York, NY 10003, (212) 674-1163 (phone), (212) 677-1981 (fax).

Questions for Dad, by Dwight Twilley, 1994, Boston: Charles E. Tuttle Company, Inc., author describes in detail a creative method for parents and children living apart to communicate and enhance their long distance relationships.

Advocating for Children and Families

For information about restorative justice, see the University of Minnesota's *Center for Restorative Justice & Mediation* at http://ssw.che.umn.edu/ctr4rjm/Default.html. This site provides links to many organizations and resources associated with conflict resolution, social justice, community restitution and other principles of restorative justice.

For information about sentencing issues, contact *The Sentencing Project,* 918 F Street, NW, Suite 501, Washington, DC 20004, (202) 628-0871, or visit online at www.sentencingproject.org. The Sentencing Project provides resources and information about criminal justice policy and program issues, including those related to alternative sentencing. Policy reports and fact sheets can be downloaded from the website.

Fathers in Prison and their Children: Visiting Policy Guidelines, Creasie Finney Hairston, Ph.D, Social Policy and Research Notes, March, 1996, Jane Addams College of Social Work.

Incarcerated Mothers and the Maintenance of Family Ties, The Subcommittee on Women, Council of the City of New York, City Hall, New York, NY, 10007, (212) 788-7250, June 21, 1996, Report summarizes four-hour hearing focused on the ability of incarcerated mothers in New York to maintain a positive relationship with their children while detained or incarcerated. Includes 35 recommendations for improving the maintenance of family ties.

Recent Media Attention

As Inmate Population Grows, So Does Focus on Children, Fox Butterfield, The New York Times, April 7, 1999, p. A1.

A Painful Parting for Prisoners: DC's Female Inmates Confront Separation from Family as Transfers Begin, Cheryl W. Thompson, The Washington Post, January 7, 1998, p. B1.

An Addict Who Is a Father, Too: Facing a Daily Struggle to Stay Clean and Keep His Children, David Rohde, The New York Times, June 14, 1998, p. A1.

Mothers in Prison, Children in Limbo, Mireya Navarro, The New York Times, July 18, 1994.

Criminal and Welfare Rules Raise New Issues of Fairness, Nina Bernstein, The New York Times, August 20, 1996, p. A1.

Percentage of Women in Criminal Population Is Rising, Justice Dept. Report Says, The Washington Post, August 18, 1997, p. A13.

F. Information about CJS and CWS Collaboration

Partnerships Between Corrections and Child Welfare: Part Two, Collaboration for Change, developed by the Women's Prison Association & Home, Inc., From the Family to Family, Tools for Rebuilding Foster Care series, published by the Annie E. Casey Foundation, 1998, Annie E. Casey Foundation, 701 Paul Street, Baltimore, MD, 21202, (410) 547-6600 (phone), (410) 547-6624 (fax), www.aecf.org.

A Guide to New York's Criminal Justice System and A Guide to New York's Child Welfare System, developed by the Women's Prison Association and South Brooklyn Legal Services, Family Law Unit. These guides were designed as cross-training manuals for New York child welfare professionals and criminal justice professionals. For more information, contact the Women's Prison Association, 110 Second Avenue, New York, NY, 10003, (212) 674-1163.

Children, Families and Correctional Supervision: Current Policies and New Directions, 1996, Creasie Finney Hairston, PhD, Shonda Wills, MSW, Nancy Wall, MSW. A report on a forum sponsored by the Jane Addams Center for Social Policy and Research which sought to explore the impact of criminal justice and child welfare policies on families affected by incarceration.

When a Mother is Arrested: How the Criminal Justice and Child Welfare Systems Can Work Together More Effectively (A Needs Assessment Initiated by the Maryland Department of Human Resources), 1996, prepared by the Women's Prison Association. This needs assessment provides one model for child welfare agencies wishing to enhance services to children with incarcerated parents and to develop more collaborative relationships with the criminal justice system. For more information, contact the Women's Prison Association, 110 Second Avenue, New York, NY, 10003, (212) 674-1163.

Cross-System Collaboration: Tools That Work, James L. Hoel, Child Welfare League of America, 1998. Not specific to incarceration. A "toollbox" of effective principles for collaboration.

About the Authors

Cynthia B. Seymour, JD, is the General Counsel of the Child Welfare League of America. In addition to her duties as legal counsel, she coordinates CWLA's Children with Parents in Prison Initiative. As part of that initiative, she authored an issue brief entitled *Parents in Prison: Children in Crisis* and an article entitled *Children with Parents in Prison: Child Welfare Policy, Program and Practice Issues.* In addition, she co-edited a special edition of CHILD WELFARE focused on children with parents in prison. Ms. Seymour received her law degree from Washington University, St. Louis.

Dr. Lois E. Wright is the assistant dean of the College of Social Work at the University of South Carolina and the director of The Center for Child and Family Studies. In this capacity, she has received funding for over one hundred grants and contracts for research and training related to children and family services. Dr. Wright received a master of science degree in social work from the Virginia Commonwealth University and a doctorate in education from the College of William and Mary. She has more than thirty years of experience in the field of social work, and she has presented at national meetings on topics such as program evaluation, family preservation services, child neglect, and agency management.